START STRONG

A NEW BELIEVER'S GUIDE TO CHRISTIANITY

KRISAN MAROTTA

EZRA'S PATH

First Edition January 2026.

Ezra's Path Publishing, Charlottesville, VA

Editor: Paul Higgins

Cover Design: 100 Covers

Interior Design: Ezra's Path Publishing

ISBN: 979-8-9997508-0-8 (ebook)

ISBN: 979-8-999-7508-1-5 (print)

ISBN: 979-8-999-7508-3-9 (hardback)

To my grandchildren:
May you come to know the One
who calls you by name,
walk with him all your days,
and finish strong in faith.

CONTENTS

Introduction　　　　　　　　　　　　　　　　vii

Part I
FACING THE TRUTH

1. Sin　　　　　　　　　　　　　　　　　　3
   The Problem We Can't Ignore
2. Guilt　　　　　　　　　　　　　　　　　15
   Why Good Intentions Are Not Enough
3. The Cross　　　　　　　　　　　　　　　23
   Why Jesus Had to Die
4. Faith　　　　　　　　　　　　　　　　　30
   What it Means to Trust Jesus

Part II
LIVING THE TRUTH

5. A New Way of Seeing　　　　　　　　　47
   God at the Center
6. The Church　　　　　　　　　　　　　59
   Finding Your New Family
7. Daily Life　　　　　　　　　　　　　　65
   What Following Jesus Looks Like
8. Trials　　　　　　　　　　　　　　　　80
   How God Uses Hard Times

Part III
CONFRONTING THE LIES

9. Holiness　　　　　　　　　　　　　　93
   Learning to Desire What's Good
10. Sex　　　　　　　　　　　　　　　　103
    Trusting God with Desire
11. Work　　　　　　　　　　　　　　　109
    Serving God in Daily Life
12. Money　　　　　　　　　　　　　　118
    Trusting God, Not Wealth

Part IV
FINISHING STRONG
13. The Holy Spirit   125
  Your Helper in the Christian Life
14. Hope   139
  Holding On Until the End
15. Eight Truths to Remember   148
  A Note at the End   157
  Reader and Leader Extras   159
  Acknowledgments   161
  Glossary   163
  About the Author   173

INTRODUCTION

You're not crazy, and you're not alone.

If you've recently started following Jesus, you may feel like you've stepped into the middle of a movie without knowing the plot. Everyone else seems to know the lines, the music, where to stand, and what happens next.

You're trying to pay attention, but inside you're secretly thinking: *How do I make sense of this and where do I begin? How do I catch up when I feel so far behind?* That's where this book can help.

If you're reading this, chances are you've recently decided to follow Jesus, or you're seriously thinking about it, and you're wondering how to start.

Maybe you hit rock bottom, prayed a prayer and reached out to God. Maybe you were moved by a friend's faith. Perhaps someone who cares about you slipped this book into your hands because they want to spend eternity with you.

Whatever brought you here, you probably have questions like: *What does the Bible say? What does it look like to follow Jesus? How is my life supposed to change? Am I really saved?*

If you've been asking questions like these, you're not alone. And you're in the right place.

This book is your starting point. It won't answer every question, but it can give you a framework for understanding the essentials. Think of it as a trusted guide to help you begin the most important journey of your life: the journey of faith. Step by step, we'll walk through what it means to believe, to grow, and to live as a follower of Jesus.

The goal is simple: to help you start strong and keep going with wisdom and confidence.

WHAT YOU NEED TO BEGIN

All you need is a willingness to learn and a Bible. That's it. You can use a physical Bible, read it online, or download an app, whatever works best for you.

I'll be quoting the English Standard Version (ESV) because it is clear and faithful to the original text. But any version you understand and enjoy is fine.

If you've never read the Bible before, I suggest avoiding paraphrased versions for now (like *The Message* or *The Living Bible*). You want something that stays closer to what the original authors said (like the *English Standard Version* or the *New American Standard Bible*).

For the best experience, read this book with a trusted Christian friend or a small group. It's helpful to have someone to discuss these ideas with as you learn. You can download a set of free discussion questions for each chapter.

If you prefer taking notes, there's a companion workbook to help you reflect on, respond to, and apply what you're learning.

And, if after reading the chapter, you'd like to explore the topic more, you can listen to my companion podcast where I explain one of the See for Yourself passages at the end of each chapter.

You can find all these resources at startstrongbook.org.

HOW THIS BOOK IS DIFFERENT

Maybe someone already gave you advice like find a church, join a small group, pray, and read your Bible. That's good advice. You don't need to finish this book before acting on it.

Find a Bible-teaching church, attend in person, join a small group in that church, pray and read your Bible.

Maybe you're reading this book as part of a church class. Or maybe you're still looking for a church home and wondering where to begin. Most churches have websites where you can listen to sermons and find the information you need to plan your visit. You can also ask Christian friends for recommendations. You likely have more around you than you realize.

Don't worry, you don't need to be perfect or have everything figured out to show up at church. No one else does. Churches are filled with other repentant sinners, just like you and me.

This book doesn't provide advice on how to find a church, study your Bible, or pray. It's a guide to help you understand the foundational truths of the Christian worldview.

Instead of telling you which steps to take, it will walk you through the core convictions that shape the Christian faith. You won't find these truths tucked away in one corner of the Bible. They're woven throughout all of Scripture, forming the backbone of everything else.

Think of these truths like baking a cake. Every recipe starts with key ingredients like butter, sugar, and flour. If you mix them up, say you use salt instead of sugar, it doesn't matter how carefully you follow the rest of the instructions, the cake won't turn out right.

These core truths of Christianity work the same way. When you start with the right foundation, the entire building stands solid and sturdy. But if you misunderstand the essentials, the Bible can sound like it's saying things it never meant to say.

With such a big topic, you might wonder why there are so

few chapters. The Bible is a vast book, but it is also remarkably consistent. The same core truths appear again and again, taught from different angles, repeated in different stories, and reinforced through different voices.

My goal isn't to cover every angle. It's to give you a strong foundation. That's why I've chosen the main themes that are woven throughout all of Scripture. Once you understand these, new books and passages of the Bible will begin to feel more familiar and less overwhelming.

∼

A Little About Me

I'm not big on long introductions. When I read a book, I want to get straight to the point. But you may be curious about who's writing this book and why you should trust her. So here's a bit of my story.

If you'd rather dive right in, feel free to skip to the next section.

I grew up in an atheist home. As I approached high school graduation, I started asking big life questions like: What am I going to do with my life? What really matters?

I didn't have any answers. But some of my Christian friends did. They invited me to *Youth for Christ*, where I eventually prayed a sinner's prayer and became a Christian.

But I knew almost nothing about Christianity. I couldn't even tell you who Noah was. (If you don't know either, there's a glossary in the back of the book.)

The Bible felt like a giant puzzle with no edge pieces. I had no idea where to start.

Friends told me to start by reading one of the Gospels, so I did. But Jesus' words made no sense to me. I related more to the Pharisees than anyone else, and they were clearly the bad guys.

I felt lost and confused, and worse, I was afraid to admit it. My Christian friends seemed to have it all together, and I didn't want to sound foolish. I had too many questions and not enough answers.

College changed everything. I found a church that not only told me what the Bible said, but also taught me how to study it for myself.

Two years after that first prayer, my college pastor taught Romans 5–8 at a retreat. He walked through the gospel from beginning to end. For the first time, I understood some core basic truths. God's story made sense, and I could finally see it.

That retreat was a turning point. It was like he handed me a map and said, "This is where you are. Here's where you're going. Let's walk this together." That moment lit a fire in me, a passion for studying Scripture that hasn't gone out since.

I've always loved learning. (Yes, I was that kid who actually liked homework because it meant discovering something new.) When I don't have something new to explore, I get restless.

The Bible is a treasure trove. Every time I study it, I find something I haven't seen before. Bible study is a journey that never gets old, and one I want to invite you into.

After college, I followed that same pastor to a new school he was launching devoted to learning how to study the Bible. I spent three years there in a graduate-level program, learning biblical Greek, Hebrew, and exegesis (that's a fancy word for digging into what the biblical text means).

Since then, I've continued learning, decade after decade, spending twenty to twenty-five hours a week in the Scriptures. I'm still a student at heart. But after forty years of this deep, consistent work, I've learned a few things worth sharing.

For over twenty years, I taught a weekly Bible study at my church, slowly working through books of the Bible with anyone who wanted to learn. In 2011, I launched the Wednesday in the

Word podcast to share those teachings more widely. By 2019, it had become my full-time ministry.

And in 2025, after retiring from my day job, I finally had the time to add something I had long hoped to do: write books like this one. Teaching has always been at the heart of what I do, whether in person, behind a microphone, or now, on the page.

Today, biblical illiteracy is more common than ever, even among people who attend church. Many sincere believers have not learned how to study the Bible or how the core messages of Christianity fit together. They may know a few familiar stories or favorite verses, but they've never seen how the central themes work together.

That's part of the reason I wrote this book. Whether you're new to the faith or have been around it for a while, you can benefit from a clear, trustworthy foundation. No hype. No shortcuts. Just solid teaching that lays a strong foundation for a lifetime of faith.

Sometimes I answer Bible questions on Reddit, and one question comes up again and again: "Help! I'm a new Christian, and I don't know where to start." I typed out the same advice so many times, I finally thought, I should just write this down.

That's how this book began. This is the book I wish someone had handed me when I first believed, something that laid out the core truths of the gospel clearly and simply.

When I first started learning, it felt like I was learning random truths here and there with no organization or connection. I caught a few ideas, but I didn't know what had come before or how they fit together. I longed for someone to lay the foundation so I could build on it with confidence, knowing I was standing on something solid.

That's what I hope this book becomes for you: a place to start strong.

FINAL THOUGHTS

You can learn this. I'm not a genius or a scholar in an ivory tower. If I figured it out (with help from mentors and teachers), so can you.

You don't need a theology degree or a shelf full of commentaries.

You just need a Bible, some curiosity, and the willingness to keep asking questions until you understand.

If you've put your trust in Jesus, welcome to God's family. I'm so glad you're here, and I'm honored to walk this journey with you.

If you're still considering that step, I pray you'll find the answers you're seeking. Let's start at the beginning together.

PART I

FACING THE TRUTH

SIN

THE PROBLEM WE CAN'T IGNORE

For the wages of sin is death, but the free gift of God is eternal life in Christ Jesus our Lord.

— ROMANS 6:23

I f you asked most people what the Bible is about, they'd probably say God's love. And that's true. God's love is a central theme. But it's not the primary subject. The Bible focuses on a deeper and more uncomfortable topic: our sin and God's response to it.

I suspect that if you counted, you'd find more verses about our sin than about God's love. That's not because God's love isn't important; it is.

But until we understand the problem of sin, we can't begin to grasp the depth of God's love. The first step in our faith journey is repentance, which means turning away from sin and turning toward God.

THE CRACKED MIRROR

Imagine that as you're getting ready for an important event, you glance at yourself in a mirror. A crack splinters the mirror right down the middle. No matter how carefully you straighten your tie or how precisely you apply your makeup, your reflection stays distorted.

The crack in the mirror conceals the actual problems from your view. You can't fix what you see because you can't see the problem clearly.

Sin distorts like a cracked mirror.

It warps how we see everything: our relationships, our desires, our purpose, and even our understanding of God. We misjudge what's good and overvalue what won't last. We misunderstand who God is and who we are.

And like a broken mirror, no amount of surface adjustment can fix the deeper problem. We will continue to see a warped version of reality until God replaces the "mirror" by healing our sin and renewing our minds.

That's why the Bible doesn't highlight love songs or warm affirmations. It emphasizes the problem of sin.

Unless we understand that our "mirror" is broken, we'll never understand how much we need the One who came to fix it.

THE TURN AROUND

Matthew, one of Jesus' twelve apostles, summarized what Jesus taught in a single phrase: "Repent, for the kingdom of heaven is at hand" (Matthew 4:17). That one word, repent, is at the heart of the Christian life.

But what does it actually mean? For many of us, the word

can feel heavy or confusing. Does it mean saying we're sorry and trying harder to be good? Is it about feeling guilty enough to earn forgiveness? Or cleaning ourselves up before coming to God?

Some of us think that repentance is a one-time feeling, something we do at conversion and then move past. Others associate it with shame, fear, or condemnation.

To repent means to completely change direction.

Repentance differs from guilt or regret. It's a decisive shift, a reorientation of the will, heart, and mind.

For instance, say that you're following GPS directions, confident that you're on the right road. But then you realize that you're headed north when you should be going south.

It doesn't matter how far you've driven; you're traveling the wrong way. If you want to reach your destination, you need to stop, turn around, and go the other way. That's repentance.

The journey of faith begins by turning around and following a new road. But in order to turn around, we have to understand both what we're turning *from* and what we're turning *toward*. Without that clarity, repentance may simply become a slight adjustment, like veering a few degrees off our current course, when what we need is an entirely new map.

WHEN THE WORLD FELL APART

Imagine your life as a house that you built with your own hands. You admire the solid oak beams, the bright white paint, the roof that gleams in the sun. You step back, satisfied. It's strong. It's beautiful. Confident that it will stand, you leave it behind to take a job in the big city.

But when you return, something's changed. The paint is peeling, the roof has a leak, and the walls are cracking. Weeds and vines have crept up the outside. Bugs have taken over the inside. What once felt solid now feels fragile and desperately in need of repair.

That's the nature of life in a broken world. Left alone, everything falls apart. Chaos creeps in when we stop working to maintain order.

Science calls this entropy. Entropy measures the level of disorder in a system. A clean room has low entropy because everything is in its place. A messy room has high entropy because its contents are scattered in disarray.

The messy room never cleans itself. If left alone, it only gets worse. Someone has to step in and exert energy to put things right.

The same is true of our souls. Left to ourselves, we drift and decay. If no one intervenes, the mess gets worse.

Entropy is sin's footprint.

Because of sin, everything in creation fights a constant, losing battle against disorder. Left on its own, the world slides from order to chaos, from life to death, from clean to corrupt, and from whole to broken. That's what Scripture means when it speaks of death.

When the New Testament talks about death, it means more than just the end of life. Physical death is part of it, of course, but the concept goes deeper.

Death also includes this principle of entropy. It involves the slow, ongoing process of decay and corruption that touches every part of our world.

We see it everywhere: trees fall, mountains erode, cities crumble into ruins. Even the strongest structures and most brilliant inventions eventually wear out. No matter how hard we work to preserve and protect, nothing lasts forever.

That's the reality of life in a fallen world. The New Testament describes this physical unraveling as death or one of its synonyms, such as decay, futility, and corruption (Romans 8:20–21).

But entropy isn't just part of the physical world. It also permeates our relationships and our moral choices. Marriages fall apart, families break down, friendships dissolve, offices are overrun with politics, and nations go to war.

Left unattended, even our closest bonds begin to fray. No matter how much we desire peace and unity, our relationships deteriorate unless we actively fight against selfishness, pride, and anger.

That's the human condition. The world is locked in a constant battle with physical, relational, and spiritual entropy: not just because things wear out, but because we corrupt it. We are sinful, and sin corrupts everything we touch.

Sin entered the world when the first humans rebelled against God, a moment we now call the Fall (Genesis 3). From that point on, sin corrupts every person born into this world. We often think of sin as breaking one of God's rules, and that's certainly part of it.

But sin runs deeper. It includes both failing to do what's right, and doing what is good for the wrong reason. We can sin by actively mistreating others, and we can also sin by simply failing to act.

At its core, sin is a posture of the heart.

It says "no" to God and "yes" to the self. It puts me and what I value at the center. While it may chase good things like security, comfort, pleasure, or prosperity, it chases them on *my* terms, in *my* own way, not caring if I harm others or dishonor God.

Sometimes sin is obvious and destructive: lying, cheating, stealing, or abuse. At other times, it hides behind good intentions: pride in our own goodness, a critical spirit masked as discernment, or a desire to control others in the name of love. But at the root, sin always claims to know better than God and others.

The apostle Paul puts it plainly: "The wages of sin is death" (Romans 6:23). Not maybe. Not sometimes. Always. Sin causes death the way gravity causes objects to fall. Drop your phone, and it hits the floor every time.

Sin works the same way. When we sin, something breaks. Maybe it's a relationship or a lost opportunity. Maybe it creates a quiet wedge between us and God.

Sin always has consequences.

Even when no one else sees, sin leaves its mark. We see it in problems like anger, bitterness, jealousy, frustration, loss, or regret.

Because every human being is a sinner, we all live with the effects of sin and death every day. Just look around: the world is full of lies, corruption, injustice, violence, hatred, greed, and fear. We don't need to look far to see it.

RIPPLE EFFECT

Sin doesn't miss a soul, and sin never stays contained. It spreads like ripples from a stone dropped into a still pond, sending wave after wave across the surface. The bigger the stone, the wider the ripples. But even small stones disturb the water.

Picture a husband who cheats on his wife. Death doesn't begin with the divorce papers. It starts quietly long before that, with small lies, missed dinners, and emotional distance. Then come the cover-ups and angry, frustrated fights.

When the truth finally surfaces, the family begins to unravel. Trust is shattered. Conversations become accusations. The truth leaves the wife and children reeling, angry, confused, and insecure. *Was it my fault? Why wasn't I enough for him to stay? Did Dad leave because of me?*

Grandparents step in with casseroles and weary smiles, trying to hold things together. Friends feel torn, unsure of what to say or which side to take. Holidays change. Traditions break. Years later, after they sign the paperwork and sell the house, the echoes remain. A single betrayal sends shock waves through the entire family. One sin causes a multitude of wounds.

This is true of all sin, whether it's public or private, dramatic or hidden. Sin leaves destruction in its wake. Sometimes we see the damage right away; at other times, it takes years to show.

But the effect is always there. That's why repentance matters so deeply. It's not just about being sorry. It's about recognizing the harm, turning back to God, and allowing him to begin the work of restoration.

HOPE ON THE HORIZON

This may be starting to feel grim. But the story doesn't stop with sin. When we repent, sin is what we're turning from. But we are turning toward hope.

Repentance is more than running from the wreckage; it's racing toward something breathtakingly wonderful.

Paul didn't stop with, "the wages of sin is death." The sentence continues, "but the free gift of God is eternal life in Christ Jesus our Lord" (Romans 6:23).

Just as death is more than no longer breathing, the promise of eternal life is more than living forever. In the kingdom of heaven, the moral entropy of our world will be reversed. Death will be undone. Decay will be replaced by flourishing. We will be governed by fulfillment instead of futility.

In heaven, we will be transformed into people who naturally

embrace what is good and enhance what is right. No longer will we destroy life through selfishness, evil, or ignorance.

Instead, we'll nurture and uphold the goodness around us. We will be what we were always meant to be: whole, restored, fully alive. Not only will we humans be redeemed, creation will also be free from corruption.

A City With No Locks

Imagine a world without sin: no war, betrayal, or tragedy. Families flourish. Relationships are fulfilling and whole. No one locks their doors because there is nothing to fear. All work is meaningful. Everyone tells the truth.

People are caring and generous, including you. Everything that you do adds to the beauty around you, not because you're trying hard, but because it's who you are.

That's eternal life, not only unending life, but unending life that is holy, which means it is no longer marred by sin, death, decay, futility, or corruption.

> Just as sin inevitably leads to death, holiness inevitably leads to life.

That pattern is also woven into creation itself. And the incredible gift of God is that we don't have to wait for all of it. Even now, in the middle of a broken world, God gives us a taste of the life to come. As we grow in faith, wisdom, and righteousness, we begin to experience a bit of the life we were created for.

This isn't a fairy tale. It's the kingdom of heaven—and it is coming. When Jesus returns, he will conquer death once and for all and establish justice and righteousness over all creation. No more lies. No more tears. No more death and decay (Revelation 21:4).

Instead, we'll live in a world so alive you can feel it, every breath humming with joy. He has promised it: a new creation where we're not just survivors; we are holy, radiant, and eternal.

This is the hope of the gospel. It's worth waiting for. As Jesus taught in the parable of the pearl of great price, it's worth losing everything in this world to gain it (Matthew 13:44–46).

When we repent, we're not just turning from sin; we're running toward eternal life, joy, and peace.

～

THREE LIES WE LIVE BY

Since sin leads to death and holiness leads to life, why doesn't everyone repent right away? It is because we don't see clearly. Scripture tells us that we look at the world through the cracked, distorted mirror of sin. We believe three colossal lies that keep us from recognizing our need for repentance.

1. We lie about God.

God is our all-powerful, holy, and merciful Creator. He made us. He sustains us and he calls us to worship, trust, and obey him. We owe him everything.

But instead of honoring him, we ignore him. We blame him for what goes wrong in our lives or pretend he isn't there at all. We live as if his will doesn't matter and as if we are the ones in charge.

But Scripture reminds us that the day is coming when each of us will stand before God and give an account. Denying God doesn't make him disappear. It only blinds us to the truth that he is both our Creator and Judge.

11

2. We lie about ourselves.

We like to think we're basically good people, flawed maybe, but decent. We compare ourselves to others and think, *Sure, I've made some mistakes, but I'm better than most.*

But deep down, we know that we're not as good as we should be. We are wired for self-interest. We say hurtful things, act out of pride, and trample others when it benefits us.

If we're honest, we'd recognize we are deeply sinful. No amount of volunteering, church attendance, or good intentions can erase our guilt before a holy God. Until we admit the depth of our brokenness, we'll never see our need for grace.

3. We lie about the world.

This world is broken. It's ruled by death, tragedy, frustration, and futility. But we convince ourselves that something in it can still make us happy. We chase success, pleasure, comfort, or control, believing that if we just try harder, we can make life work.

But the more we chase, the more restless we become. The world cannot deliver what it promises because it is corrupted by sin. It's cracked at the foundation, and no amount of effort on our part can fix what sin has broken.

Only Jesus can bring genuine change and lasting fulfillment. Until we stop clinging to this world's empty promises, we'll keep missing the one promise that is actually guaranteed.

LAST CALL BEFORE THE WATERFALL

Imagine you're on a party boat under a clear blue sky. The sunshine glints off the river like liquid glass around you. A soft breeze carries the scent of wildflowers, weaving through the gentle strum of a guitar as your friends' laughter dances in the air. Life feels unstoppable.

Then you hear a distant noise. Turning your head, you realize you are heading directly for a massive waterfall. In an instant, the party feels small. The music fades and the fun becomes a flimsy mask.

You see the danger now. You no longer believe the lie that this party is all there is. Suddenly, nothing matters more than turning that boat around before it's too late.

Recognizing our own sinfulness and God's coming judgment is like spotting a waterfall in our path. Many people keep partying, ignoring the warning signs. They convince themselves that it isn't serious, that judgment isn't real, and that there will be plenty of time to consider such things later.

But once the truth breaks through, once you know God exists, that he is holy, and that one day you will stand before him, you can't go back to pretending.

Others may still believe that everyone goes to heaven and that Judgment Day is a myth. But once you stop lying about God, yourself, and the world, their arguments no longer seem persuasive.

History is headed toward a waterfall. Judgment Day is coming, and the most important thing you can do is to make sure that you're not swept away. Only clinging to the cross will keep you from going over the edge.

But we're not there yet. Before we can jump to safety, there's one more obstacle in our way.

SUMMARY

- Sin distorts every perception of God, self, and reality so that we cannot diagnose, much less repair, our condition without divine help.

- Repentance is the indispensable first step of faith, a total about-face in mind and will, not a fleeting emotion or mere apology.
- Sin ushers in "death" understood broadly as universal entropy: physical decay, relational breakdown, moral corruption, and spiritual alienation.
- This death principle entered the world at the Fall and now permeates all creation, ensuring that everything untended drifts from order to chaos.
- Sin is deeper than law-breaking; it is a self-centered posture that exalts personal preference over God's authority and harms others in pursuit of its own ends.
- Eternal life is not merely endless existence but a future without decay, where holiness naturally generates flourishing and joy.
- People resist repentance because sin blinds them with three great lies: denying God's rule, excusing their own guilt, and trusting the broken world to satisfy them.

SEE FOR YOURSELF

Romans 6:15–7:6; Romans 8:12–25; 1 John 1:5–10; Ephesians 2:1–10

REFLECTION

If you knew that some of your habitual choices were quietly eroding your life and relationships, what first step would you take to confront and change them? What keeps you from taking that step?

2

GUILT

WHY GOOD INTENTIONS ARE NOT ENOUGH

For all have sinned and fall short of the glory of God, and
are justified by his grace as a gift, through the redemption that is in Christ Jesus ...

— ROMANS 3:23–24

The courtroom fell silent. The defendant stood as the
guilty verdict was read. He had rehearsed his apology a
hundred times, convinced that if he just explained, if the judge
understood how sorry he was, the sentence could be reversed.

But the gavel fell anyway. Life in prison. As they led him out
in handcuffs, he replayed his mistakes, wishing he could rewrite
the past. But wishing didn't change the verdict, and remorse
couldn't undo what he had done.

Like a defendant in a trial, one day all of us will one stand
before the throne of heaven, and we will be found guilty before
God. Our apologies don't erase the past because guilt isn't
changed by regret. Guilt rests on what is true. And the truth is
we've broken something that we can't fix.

CHAINS WE FORGED OURSELVES

Sin has two devastating consequences. To understand them, we need to go back to the beginning (Genesis 1–3). In the Garden of Eden, the first humans lived face to face with God. There was no pain, no fear, no suffering, only joy, peace, and life. They walked with God in the garden, fully known and fully loved.

But then came rebellion. Humanity, represented by Adam and Eve, turned away from God and declared, "I won't live by your rules. I'll do things my way."

At its core, sin is a tragic exchange. Instead of submitting to God, we trade places with him, putting ourselves in charge. We swap truth for lies, and replace the Creator with his creation. It isn't a slight slip. It is a deliberate, willful rejection of the God who made us.

At that moment, we turned our backs on God, and sin entered the world, causing two serious problems.

DOUBLE VERDICT

Consequence 1: We are sinners.

First, we became sinners. God is the wellspring of life, holiness, and all that is good. By turning away from him, we cut ourselves off from the source of that life and goodness.

As Augustine put it, before the Fall, we had both the ability to sin and the ability not to sin. After the Fall, we lost the ability not to sin.

Our "chooser" is broken. Our chooser goes by many names such as soul, will, personality, and nature. Scripture often describes it as your heart. It is that inner faculty that determines your desires, priorities, and actions.

Now, because of sin, it chooses wrong. Or when it appears to choose right, it chooses right for the wrong reasons because it's stuck on selfish.

Because our chooser is sinful, we can't magically become perfect one day; willpower alone is insufficient. We don't simply commit sins. Sin is now part of who we are.

As we saw in the previous chapter, when sin enters, death follows every time. Our lives are now governed by a long list of evils like wickedness, greed, malice, envy, murder, strife, and deceit.

Additionally, death and entropy rule our fallen, corrupt world. It's not just that sin happens; it dominates. Like floodwaters behind a broken dam, sin rushes in and damages everything it touches. But we have an even bigger problem.

Consequence 2: We are guilty.

We are guilty before God. Our rebellion wasn't a personal failure; it was a crime. We committed treason against our Creator, and that has legal consequences.

Like the defendant in the courtroom, we may feel sorry and long to change. But sorrow doesn't erase guilt. And God, who is perfectly just, cannot overlook our crimes. The verdict is in: we are guilty, and the penalty is death.

When we turned our backs on God in rebellion, God turned his back on us in justice. Like a judge handing a convict over to begin his prison sentence, God gave us into the custody of sin. We don't just experience sin. We're trapped by it and there's no parole (Romans 1:24–28).

GUILT REQUIRES JUSTICE

At this point, you might think: *I'll just turn back to God and make things right.* But it's not that simple. Even if we want to turn back to God, God's back is still turned. We're still carrying guilt, and guilt requires justice. It doesn't go away because we say we're sorry.

This second problem (our guilt before a holy God) is even more devastating than the first. Even if we somehow found the strength to change our ways and stop sinning from this day forward, it wouldn't be enough.

Because justice demands payment for what we've already done. A righteous judge can't ignore the law, and God is a perfectly just judge.

The apostle Paul calls this second consequence the wrath of God (Romans 1:18). That phrase can sound harsh, but it's not about God flying into a rage. God's wrath is not irrational or cruel. It's the holy response of a holy God to all that is evil, corrupt, and unjust.

No Alibi

We are without excuse. We can't claim ignorance. God has made himself known through creation. The order, beauty, and complexity of the world all point to a Creator.

Imagine walking down a sidewalk and discovering a million pennies, all heads-up, laid out in perfect rows. You wouldn't think that happened by accident. You'd assume that someone placed them there on purpose.

Look at the universe. Its design is far too intentional to be random. And deep down, we know it. We know God exists, but we choose to ignore him. That's why ignorance is no excuse. We're not unaware. We're willfully blind.

Most people believe in some kind of supernatural force that stays out of our lives and rewards "good" people with heaven. But Scripture tells a different story.

When we understand guilt, we see that idea of a distant god for what it is: a comforting illusion. God is not indifferent. He is present, just, and he cares deeply about who we are and how we live. One day, we will each stand before him.

Many people think Christianity is about being a good person. Be kind, try hard, help others, go to church, and you'll be fine, right?

But that's not what the Bible says. Scripture teaches that no one is good enough. No one is even close. We can't earn our way to God by being nice or sincere.

The gospel isn't about self-improvement. It's about rescue.

> Jesus didn't come to make good people better. He came
> to save the guilty.

Why isn't being a good person enough? Because none of us is good in the way God requires. Our choosers are broken. We can't balance the scales by trying harder or following the rules.

Whether we measure ourselves by the Ten Commandments or our own moral standards, the result is the same: we fall short. Sin isn't just about what we do; it's about who we are.

BEYOND SELF-REPAIR

Selfishness taints even our best efforts. Sure, now and then we might hold our tongues, act kindly, or lend a hand, but underneath, our choosers are bent inward. God isn't only interested in our external behavior; he cares about our internal motives.

His Law not only calls us to do the right thing; it calls us to want to do the right thing. God calls us to holiness, not just rule-following. And holiness requires a pure heart, something we can not produce on our own.

Knowledge won't fix the problem either. Knowing what's right is not the same as doing it. Information alone can't transform a heart that's still enslaved to sin.

Even if we could somehow fix our broken choosers (which

we can't), we still face a deeper issue: guilt. We owe a debt we cannot repay. Justice still demands a reckoning. We need deliverance, not directions.

PARDON GRANTED

Here's the good news: God is not only just; he is also merciful. He doesn't leave us trapped in guilt, powerless to change. He made a way to deal with our problem. The Bible calls that solution justification.

> Justification is God's act of declaring us innocent,
> because someone else paid our debt for us.

The penalty for sin was real. The debt was staggering. But Jesus stepped in and paid it fully, finally, and freely.

When we put our faith in Jesus, God declares us justified. That declaration means we are no longer guilty rebels; we become beloved sons and daughters.

With our guilt removed, he metaphorically turns his face toward us, restoring our relationship, and welcoming us into his family.

This isn't a loophole or legal trick. As the guilty verdict came down on us defendants, Jesus entered the courtroom and said he would serve the sentence on our behalf.

This is the core of the gospel: a just God making a path for guilty people to receive complete forgiveness without compromising his justice or withholding his mercy.

On the cross, Jesus bore the punishment we deserved, and God accepted his sacrifice on our behalf. The resurrection proved that it worked. When we repent and trust in his sacrifice, God declares us justified. He clears our record, not because we earned it, but because Jesus paid the bill.

Not accepting Jesus is like yelling at the judge: "I don't know who this man is and he cannot stand in my place." The judge will let you do that, but you won't like the consequences.

Justification is a gift, freely given and made possible by the cross. The cross is where justice and mercy meet, because it solves both the problem of God's wrath and our guilt.

The gospel is more than simply "God loves you and has a wonderful plan for your life," though that is true. The good news of the gospel is that we were guilty, but Jesus took our punishment. We were condemned, but Jesus justified us.

There's no need to hide from God, hoping he won't notice what you've done. There's no pressure to earn your way back or balance the scales. Because Jesus stood in your place, you can stand in the light, forgiven and free.

But if you're like me, you may wonder why it had to be this way. Couldn't God have just forgiven us without all the suffering Jesus went through? Why was death the price?

These aren't minor questions. They go to the heart of the gospel, and the heart of God himself. We'll tackle them next.

SUMMARY

- Sin carries a double fallout: it corrupts our nature so that we "cannot not sin," and it renders us legally guilty before a perfectly just Judge.
- Guilt is more devastating than moral weakness, for God's righteous wrath demands payment; neither regret nor future good behavior can satisfy justice.
- The gospel is rescue, not renovation: Jesus stepped into the courtroom, bore the full sentence we deserved, and satisfied justice on the cross.
- God's act of justification declares believers innocent,

not because they are sinless, but because Christ paid our debt.

See for Yourself

Romans 1:18-32; Romans 3:1–31; Galatians 3:1–14; Psalm 51

Reflection

Since guilt is an objective debt that must somehow be settled, who or what are you counting on to pay it, and on what basis do you trust that solution?

3

THE CROSS

WHY JESUS HAD TO DIE

And you, who were dead in your trespasses and the uncircumcision of your flesh, God made alive together with him, having forgiven us all our trespasses, by canceling the record of debt that stood against us with its legal demands. This he set aside, nailing it to the cross.

— COLOSSIANS 2:13–14

I magine trying to pay off a billion-dollar debt with a minimum-wage job. You could work every hour of every day for the rest of your life, and it still wouldn't be enough.

Then, just when you've lost all hope, an uncle you barely know steps in and says, "I've got this."

Without blinking, he pays your debt in full. Just like that, you're free, not because you earned it, but because someone else intervened.

That's the cross. It's the answer to our biggest problem: our guilt before God. But why does it work? How does Jesus' death pay for our sins?

In this chapter, we'll explore why the cross is the only solution that could ever set us free. I'll also define some theological terms you can use to impress your friends (and understand your pastor).

CRUSHING DEBT

God is the one who defines right and wrong. He created us, gave us his Law, and commanded us to be holy as he is holy. But we aren't. We have broken his commands repeatedly. Even if we only sinned once, we would still be guilty. But we've gone far beyond that. Our entire lives are marred by sin.

Imagine a flawless porcelain vase, smooth, perfect, and beautiful. Now picture it smashed into pieces. You can glue it back together, but the cracks will always show. That's what sin does to us. Once we break God's Law, we can't undo it. No amount of effort can make us perfect again.

Some people try to make excuses such as "Nobody's perfect," and "God gives second chances." We have no right to another chance, and getting one wouldn't change anything. Because even if God gave us a million chances, we'd still fall short. Mercy and grace are gifts, not rewards for good effort. Sin isn't just something we do; it's who we are because our choosers are broken.

The apostle Paul compares sin in us to yeast in bread dough (1 Corinthians 5:6). When you add a teaspoon of yeast to a batch of dough, the yeast doesn't stay in one corner of the loaf. It spreads through the batch, leaving no corner of dough untouched. Sin works the same way. Theologians call this total depravity.

Total depravity means sin touches every part of us.

Total depravity does not mean we're as bad as we can possibly be. It means that sin invades every part of who we are, including our thoughts, motives, desires, and actions. There's no pure part of us we can draw from to fix ourselves. There's no hidden well of goodness we can tap. We're broken all the way through, and we owe a debt to God we can never repay.

But remember, sin is more than breaking the rules. Sin is personal. It's a betrayal of God himself. We're not the victims in this story; God is. He never wronged us or broke a promise. We are the ones who rebelled, ignored our promises, and failed to love God.

The Bible describes this idea with a striking metaphor: God is the faithful husband, and we are the unfaithful wife (Hosea 1–3; Ezekiel 16). He has always been patient and true, but we ran after other lovers like money, comfort, control, approval, and idols. Even though we broke his trust, he remained faithful.

Some people think all religions teach basically the same thing. But Christianity stands apart. It is the only religion where the answer is not some version of "try harder." Instead, God came down to rescue you, because you can't save yourself.

Christianity alone claims trying harder does not work.

Every other religion offers guidance about what you should do and how you should change. Christianity gives good news and tells you who to trust. The core message is not what you must do, but what Jesus did for you. If we could save ourselves, we wouldn't need the cross.

Paid in Full

What Jesus did is comparable to co-signing a loan. If the borrower defaults, the co-signer is legally obligated to pay the rest of the loan. Like a co-signer, Jesus agreed to pay our debt when we defaulted.

He wasn't guilty himself, but he assumed our debt and paid

it in full. He stood in for us, not just symbolically, but legally. At the cross, he bore the penalty we deserved so that we could go free. He didn't just die *for* us. He died *instead* of us.

But that raises an important question: Why was Jesus' death necessary? Couldn't God simply forgive us without demanding payment? If God is so loving and merciful, why not simply wipe the slate clean?

That's where we need to understand how justice and mercy work together and why the cross is the only way to satisfy both.

WHERE JUSTICE MEETS MERCY

When Christ agreed to pay our debt, he also became our mediator. A mediator brings two estranged parties back together. Jesus stepped in between us and God to repair the breach created by our sin.

Mediation involves two crucial ideas: satisfaction and reconciliation. By paying the penalty for our sin on the cross, Jesus satisfied justice. With justice satisfied, God can forgive us so that we can be reconciled to him and adopted as his children.

God's anger over sin is not a popular topic today. Many modern churches would rather leave the doctrine of God's wrath locked away in a theological closet.

But Scripture speaks often and clearly about the wrath of God (Exodus 34:6–9; Psalm 7; Ephesians 5:1–6; Colossians 3:5–6; John 3:36). God despises evil. His wrath is a just and holy response to sin.

Some people picture God as angry and eager to catch us doing something wrong. But that's not the God of the Bible. Yes, God is just, and he takes sin seriously. But he's not eager to punish. Scripture says God is "slow to anger and abounding in steadfast love" (Exodus 34:6).

His anger is not like ours. It's not a short fuse or a bad mood.

It's a holy response to our evil. He hates what destroys us, but his goal isn't destruction. It's restoration.

He sent his son because he wanted to save us, not crush us. The cross shows us that God's love and justice are not in conflict. They work together for our rescue.

But here's a key concept: God wasn't obligated to accept that exchange. As the one wronged, God had every right to make us pay the debt ourselves. But in an astounding act of mercy and grace, he accepted Christ's death on our behalf.

His justice demands that sin be punished. His mercy desires to forgive sinners. On the cross, both justice and mercy are fulfilled.

The cross is the price of justice and the proof of mercy.

This explains why the Bible calls Jesus' death a ransom (Mark 10:45). In the ancient world, a ransom was the payment required to set a slave or a prisoner of war free. The slaveholder, the conquering general, or the person wronged sets the price of the ransom. Once the price is set, a redeemer decides if he will pay it.

The theological terms that help us understand this ransom are substitution and satisfaction. Substitution means that Jesus took the punishment we deserved. Satisfaction means that his sacrifice met the demands of God's justice. Together, they describe what Scripture calls Christ's atoning sacrifice.

Atonement is a legal term. It means making amends or compensating for a wrong.

To atone is to take responsibility and pay the penalty to satisfy justice.

When we say that Christ's death was an atoning sacrifice, we mean Jesus paid the debt we owed. His death satisfied the justice of God and cleared the way for our forgiveness.

And here's the incredibly good news: we didn't deserve any of it. God wasn't required to sacrifice his son. Jesus wasn't obligated to die for us. Justice could have fallen on us, and it would have been fair.

But God loved us enough to send his son, and Jesus loved us enough to take our place. That's what makes grace so amazing.

But there's still one more question we have to ask: If Jesus' death was enough to pay for everyone's sin, does that mean everyone is automatically saved? The answer is no, not everyone is justified. There is one essential condition. We will look at that in the next chapter.

SUMMARY

- Total depravity means sin touches every thought, motive, and action, leaving no "good part" from which to repair ourselves.
- Christianity differs from all "try-harder" religions by announcing rescue, not self-reform: God himself enters history to pay the debt we can never clear.
- On the cross, Jesus became our legal substitute, assuming our guilt and exhausting God's righteous wrath so that justice would be satisfied and mercy released.
- Christ's death is both ransom and atoning sacrifice: he took the punishment we deserved (substitution) and fully met the Law's demands (satisfaction), canceling the record of debt against us.
- God's wrath is neither capricious nor cruel; it is the necessary, holy response to evil, yet his steadfast love

moved him to accept Christ's payment instead of
demanding ours.

- The cross therefore unites justice and mercy, showing
  God to be perfectly righteous while freely justifying
  those who trust in Jesus.

SEE FOR YOURSELF

Isaiah 53:7–12; Colossians 2:4–15; John 3:16–21; Hebrews
9:11–28.

REFLECTION

If someone truly absorbed the full cost of every wrong you've
ever done, leaving you nothing to repay, how might that alter
the way you view both your past failures and your future
choices?

4

FAITH

WHAT IT MEANS TO TRUST JESUS

For by grace you have been saved through faith. And this is not your own doing; it is the gift of God, not a result of works, so that no one may boast.

— EPHESIANS 2:8–9

We've seen the problem: Our sin separates us from God. We've seen the solution: Jesus took our punishment on the cross. But does that mean everyone is automatically saved? No, the Bible teaches that only those who have saving faith will receive eternal life (John 3:16; John 14:6; Ephesians 2:8–9; Romans 10:9).

But what exactly is saving faith? What must you have to enter the kingdom of heaven and receive eternal life? And how do you know if you have it? In this chapter, we'll answer these questions.

First, we'll talk about what saving faith is not, to clear up some common misunderstandings. Then we'll explore what saving faith is, and how it changes your life.

People use the word faith in many ways. We talk about

having faith in ourselves, keeping the faith during hard times, or simply having faith that everything will work out in the end. That type of ordinary, mundane faith is not what saves us.

The Bible is specific about the type of faith that saves, and it's not as vague or general as people often assume. Here's what saving faith is not.

NOT ALL FAITH SAVES

Saving faith is not positive thinking.

You've probably heard claims like, "Believe in yourself and you can do anything," or, "It's enough to believe some kind of higher power is looking out for you." Those comforting messages make great motivational speeches. But it's not what the Bible means by saving faith.

Saving faith is not self-confidence or optimism.

The Bible never says, "Just believe, and everything will be fine." That concept is wishful thinking. God is not our personal cheerleader, and faith is not a mindset we adopt to attract good things into our lives.

Saving faith is also not blind hope.

Sometimes people say it doesn't matter what you believe, as long as you believe it sincerely. In this view of faith, it's not about whether something is true; it's about how firmly you believe it. But that's not saving faith.

The Bible never encourages us to believe something that isn't true. In fact, it warns us repeatedly not to be deceived by lies. Believing without reason isn't faith; it's foolish. Saving faith is not a leap into the dark; it's a step into the light. It's rooted in the solid reality of who Jesus is and what he did on the cross.

Saving faith is not obedience either.

This idea can be tricky, because the Christian life involves obedience. Those who trust God will seek to follow him. But obedience results from faith. It is not the same thing as saving faith itself.

Some people think of faith as a kind of loyalty, like being on God's team and trying hard to live the way he expects you to live. But our efforts to obey, as good and important as they are, do not save us. Obedience flows from saving faith, not the other way around.

Neither is saving faith knowing the Bible.

You can study Scripture, get all the right answers on a theology test, and still miss the heart of the gospel. Of course, we should believe what is true and avoid false doctrine. While knowing the truth matters, knowledge alone does not save us.

Knowing that Jesus died and rose again is not the same as trusting him. Understanding the concept of salvation is not the same as believing it so much it changes your life. You can know what is true and still ignore it. Saving faith goes beyond facts and knowledge. It's about trust.

Saving faith is more than believing that God exists.

Even demons believe that and they shudder (James 2:19). Belief alone isn't the full picture. Saving faith is more than simply acknowledging that there must be "something out there" or feeling spiritual from time to time. Lots of people have a vague sense that a higher power exists, but that's not the same as trusting in the God of the Bible.

Finally, neither is saving faith trusting Jesus to fix your circumstances, make you comfortable, or ensure a tranquil life. While it's good and right to bring your daily concerns to God, that's not what saves you.

So if saving faith isn't positive thinking, blind hope, obedience, head knowledge, feeling spiritual, or belief in a higher power, what is it?

SAVING FAITH

Saving faith is an ongoing, personal trust in Jesus Christ as your only hope for salvation.

Saving faith is not about help for today. It's about hope for eternity.

One common way to explain faith is to imagine you're drowning in a stormy sea. Waves crash over your head and there is no land in sight. You're exhausted, out of strength, and going under.

Then a lifeguard pulls up on a jet ski, hauls you up behind him, and says, "Hold on tight. I've got you."

Saving faith is not believing the lifeguard exists or swimming harder, hoping you can make it on your own. Saving faith is letting him rescue you. It's being pulled from the water by his power, not yours.

Saving faith itself is a gift from God.

We don't earn it, deserve it, or create it on our own. It's not that we mustered up some faith, and God responded by saving us. Rather in his mercy, God made the first move. He sent his son to satisfy justice and to create a way to escape death. All he asks is that we trust him, and even that trust is something he gives us.

FOUR CONVICTIONS OF SAVING FAITH

Saving faith has four core convictions, which I define using the acronym R.E.A.L.:

R: RECOGNIZE YOUR SIN

The first conviction of saving faith is knowing you are sinful and longing to be different. Saving faith begins with honesty and repentance.

Instead of pretending we're basically good, we admit the truth. No more excusing sin or blaming others. We face the reality that we have rebelled against God and are deeply in the wrong.

But faith is more than feeling guilty or ashamed. It's a heart-level grief over sin, not over getting caught and facing the consequences, but over the sin itself. We hate what God hates and long to be good and holy like he is.

Jesus called this being "poor in spirit" and "mourning" over our sins (Matthew 5:3–4). It's a deep awareness that we are broken and that only God can fix us. Saving faith longs for holiness in the way a starving man longs for food.

The good news of the gospel is that those who hunger and thirst for righteousness are fortunate because they will be filled. They know they need what only God can give, and they trust God will give it (Matthew 5:6).

E: EMBRACE YOUR NEED

The second conviction of saving faith is knowing we can't save ourselves. Instead of lying to ourselves or pretending we can fix things on our own, we come to grips with reality: no amount of self-effort, good deeds, or religious devotion can cancel our guilt. There's no bargaining with God or balancing the scales.

As slaves to sin and prisoners of death, we don't need more willpower or a better plan. We need rescue. Embracing that truth frees us to stop striving to save ourselves and start trusting the One who already paid the price.

A: ACCEPT GOD'S GRACE

The third conviction of saving faith is knowing God is not required to save us. Here we stop lying about God. He doesn't owe us salvation. He's not obligated to forgive us because we tried hard or meant well. We are guilty and deserve his judgment. No amount of obedience can earn his favor. We have no divine spark he's required to honor.

Salvation is a free, entirely undeserved gift. God saves us not because we've done something right, but because he is merciful. That's the miracle of grace: we're not saved because of who we are; we're saved because of who God is.

L: LEAN ON JESUS.

This is where it all comes together. Because of the first three convictions—because we recognize our sin, understand we can't fix it, and believe God owes us nothing—the final core conviction of saving faith is trusting that God will save and forgive us because of Jesus Christ. We don't trust him because of good deeds or our sincerity. We lean all the weight of our hope on Jesus and what he did on the cross.

Let's update our lifeguard analogy to be more precise. Imagine waking up in the hospital. Tubes snake around your arms. Machines beep steadily beside your bed. You're groggy, disoriented, trying to remember what happened.

A doctor leans in and says gently, "Welcome back. You are safe now."

You didn't call 911 or drag yourself through the emergency room doors asking for help. You didn't even realize you were dying. Someone else found you unconscious and unresponsive, and got you there in time. Your heart stopped, but they revived you.

That's a better picture of God's grace. God moves first. He revives us when we have nothing to offer. We don't save ourselves; God saves us. R.E.A.L. faith is not our achievement. It's God's gift.

One day, God will send his Messiah, Jesus of Nazareth, back to earth in glory. He will come with both judgment and mercy. On that day, God will triumph over death and establish his righteous reign over all creation. He will welcome into his kingdom all who have trusted in the mercy secured by the cross.

That's why saving faith matters so deeply. In this life, our biggest need is to solve the problem of sin, and R.E.A.L. faith is the only solution. Without saving faith, there is no justification. And without justification, there is no place in God's kingdom.

The purpose of our time in this life is not to impress God or earn our way into heaven. It's to learn to trust him. Saving faith is a profound, enduring trust that God himself nurtures in us over time.

His primary goal is not giving us a smooth life. He's building something deeper. He's forming people who have mature faith which lasts and carries us through the adversity, tragedy, and daily struggles of life in a broken world. God's plan for this life isn't just to get us through it. It's to make our faith complete.

~

FRUIT OF TRUST

There's something else you need to know about saving faith, something critically important. Saying "I believe" isn't enough. Saving faith must change how you live.

The Bible teaches two key themes about faith and works. We need to understand both, because misunderstanding either will lead us off course.

Theme #1: You are saved by faith, apart from works.

This theme is the foundation we've been building: salvation comes through faith alone, not through our effort. None of us earn our way into heaven by being good enough. We are all sinners, incapable of standing before God on our own merit. Without God's grace and the blood of Christ, we remain condemned. Salvation is a gift, not a paycheck. We don't earn it. God gives it to us.

Theme #2: Saving faith changes us.

Imagine you're trapped in a burning building. Thick smoke fills the air and you can barely see. Suddenly, a firefighter bursts through the door.

"Follow me!" he shouts. "I know the way out!"

If you truly believe him, you will follow him without hesitation. Even if you are scared or uncertain, you'll move. But if you run in the opposite direction or stay where you are, your claim to believe him doesn't mean much.

What you do reveals whether you genuinely trust him. And sometimes that might mean running into the fire.

The same is true with saving faith. What we do reveals whether we have it.

Genuine saving faith changes our daily lives.

When we trust Christ, the Holy Spirit begins fixing our broken choosers. Those changes might be slow at times, and even hard to see, but they happen.

Saving faith produces a growing sorrow over sin, a deepening hunger for holiness, and a genuine desire to obey God. It begins to shape everything about us: the way we think, the values we hold, the words we speak, and the choices we make.

As God fixes our choosers, we begin to value what God values and seek to follow what he says is right. The goal is not to change in order to be saved, but to change because we are being saved.

Does having faith mean we never sin again? No, genuine believers still stumble and fall. But over time, our choices grow wiser. Our hearts turn toward God, and the direction of our lives shift. We follow, not perfectly, but increasingly; not to earn salvation, but because we've received it.

~

SHOW-ME FAITH

The Bible teaches both themes we've been talking about: we are saved by faith alone and faith changes us. As you read through Scripture, you'll notice something that may seem contradictory at first. In some places, it says God will not judge us by our works. That's theme one: we are saved by grace alone.

But in other places, the Bible talks about being judged by our works. That's theme two: the way we live reveals whether we truly have saving faith.

You might hear people claim this means the Bible contradicts itself about faith and works. In particular, you might hear that two New Testament authors, Paul and James, disagree.

Paul says, "We're saved by faith, not works" (Galatians 3:11). James says, "Faith without works is dead" (James 2:17). At first glance, it may sound like they're arguing or contradicting each other.

But they're not fighting. They're answering two different questions. Paul answers the question, "How are we saved?" His answer is that we are saved by faith alone, not by works.

James answers the question, "What does faith look like?" His answer is that because faith actively changes your life, any "faith" that makes no difference is not real faith.

Two Teachers, One Truth

Let me give you an analogy. Imagine that a famous musician named Theo starts a new music school.

One of his instructors, Paul, tells prospective students, "Anyone can join. You don't need to be a skilled musician to join. You simply need to love music."

People from all over sign up, excited about a chance to study with Theo.

But then a man joins who clearly doesn't love music. He never practices, avoids lessons, skips the rehearsals, and even complains that music is a waste of time.

Another instructor, James, pulls this man aside and tells him, "You don't belong here."

The man protests, "But Paul said anyone can join."

James replies, "That's true. But Paul also said you must love music. If you don't love music, you're not really part of the school."

It's the same with salvation. Christians face two important questions:

- Do I need to be good enough to enter heaven? No.
- Do I need to love God and live like I trust him? Yes.

Paul was right; anyone can come to faith. There's no need to get your act together first, no spiritual resume required, and no expectation that you make a sincere effort to keep the Law before coming.

But James was also right; those who truly believe will begin to love what God loves and their lifestyles will show it.

Both Paul and James agree that claiming to believe isn't enough. Saving faith always shows itself. It changes how we think, how we speak, how we live, and what we want.

Our works don't save us, but they do reveal what we believe. They show both that we are sinners in need of grace and that we trust the one who gives it.

ABRAHAM'S EXAMPLE

The so-called dispute between James and Paul gets confusing because both Paul and James point to Abraham to prove their points.

In Genesis 15:6, God promises Abraham a son. Abraham believes, even though he and his wife Sarah are far too old to have children. God responds by declaring Abraham righteous, not because of anything Abraham did, but because he trusted God's promise.

Paul highlights this moment to teach us something foundational: we're in the same position. God also made promises to us, secured by the blood of Christ. When we believe he will keep those promises, we are justified and forgiven like Abraham.

Eventually, as God promised, Abraham and Sarah had a son named Isaac. God told them he would fulfill his promises through Isaac and only through Isaac.

But then, years later, something unexpected happened. God

tested Abraham's faith in a staggering way. He asked Abraham to sacrifice Isaac, the very son God needed to fulfill his promises. Abraham obeyed, trusting that God would still keep his word, even though it seemed impossible. At the last moment, God intervened and provided a ram in Isaac's place.

Abraham faced a gut-wrenching test of faith. Obeying God in that moment seemed to put God's very promise at risk. If Isaac died, humanly speaking, there would be no way for God to keep his word. But Abraham reasoned that if God needed Isaac to fulfill his plan, then God would raise Isaac from the dead (Hebrews 11:19).

Abraham didn't ask, "Do I understand what God is doing?" He probably didn't understand. He asked, "Do I trust that God will do what he said, no matter what?"

James points to this part of the story to make his case. He shows us that Abraham didn't just claim to believe; he acted on that belief. His faith wasn't theoretical. It wasn't a feeling or a vague sense of hope. In the middle of an impossible situation, Abraham trusted God and obeyed because he had saving faith.

Most of us may never face a test as hard as Abraham's, but we will still face choices that reveal what we believe in. Life challenges us to ask ourselves these questions every day:

- Do I believe I'm truly a sinner in need of rescue? Or do I quietly assume that I'm basically good?
- Do I believe God exists and Jesus is coming back? Or do I live as if this world is all there is?
- Do I believe that eternal life can only be found in trusting in the blood of Jesus? And will I live like all that is true?

Whether or not you realize it, the decisions you make in your everyday life answer those questions. They reveal whether you're clinging to the lifeguard or flailing alone in the storm. Saving faith is simple, yet transformative.

GRACE FOR STRUGGLERS

Before we move on, I want to clarify something important. Remember the music school analogy? You can be a member of the school even if you play terrible music. It's not about perfection. It's about love of music.

In the same way, you can belong to God and still struggle with sin. Sinning doesn't mean you're kicked out of the kingdom, and it doesn't mean your faith is fake.

Some people think that becoming a Christian means that you won't struggle with sin anymore. But that's not what Scripture teaches. Saving faith doesn't mean perfection. It means direction.

We still stumble and fall. But our choosers have changed. We want to follow God even when we fail. The difference is that now when we sin, we grieve over it. We repent. And we keep turning back to the One who saves us.

After you come to faith, your works will continue to prove two things: first, you're still a sinner in need of grace; and second, you are seeking God, even if you're doing so imperfectly.

God forgives us now, while we are still sinners. But he hasn't freed us completely from the presence and power of sin yet. That day will come when Jesus returns and sets all things right. Until then, we live in the tension between longing to be holy and not being holy yet. We stumble and struggle. Sometimes we may act like hypocrites, knowing what God desires and failing to live it out.

But here's the difference: when we fall, saving faith doesn't shrug sin off as no big deal. It grieves. It leads us to confess, to repent, and to return to God. Saving faith doesn't make us flawless; it keeps drawing us back to the cross.

James warned about a different response to sin. He wrote to people who bragged about their sins and laughed off behavior that they should have mourned. He saw no grief, no repentance, and no sign that their faith was alive. They claimed to trust God, but their lifestyle said otherwise. He urged them to draw near to God.

Paul dealt with the opposite error. He confronted those who insisted we must earn God's favor by following the Old Testament Law. He urged them to stop trusting in their rule-keeping and start trusting in Christ.

Paul and James weren't contradicting each other. They were defending the same truth while fighting on two different fronts. Saving faith is a gift of grace that changes us from the inside out. It's a gift that always leads to lifestyle change, even if imperfectly.

In the next chapters, we'll talk about what some of those changes look like.

SUMMARY

- Only those who exercise saving faith receive eternal life.
- Saving faith is a gift of grace from God, never a human achievement or a reward for moral effort.

Saving faith has four core convictions (R.E.A.L.):

- R: Recognize your sin.
- E: Embrace your need.
- A: Accept God's grace.
- L: Lean on Jesus.

- True believers know they are helpless sinners, admit they cannot fix themselves, understand God owes them nothing, and trust Jesus entirely for pardon and life.
- Saving faith always produces changes in our lifestyle.
- Paul and James do not contradict each other; Paul answers the question "How are we saved?" (by faith apart from works) while James answers the question "What does real faith look like?" (it acts on what it believes).
- Abraham illustrates both dimensions: God declared him righteous when he believed God's promise, and later Abraham proved that faith by trusting God in the test with Isaac.
- Authentic Christians still sin, but saving faith grieves over failure, repents, and keeps turning back to Christ, showing direction toward holiness rather than flawless performance.

SEE FOR YOURSELF

Matthew 5:1–16; James 2:14–26; Galatians 2:11–21; Romans 4:1–25.

REFLECTION

What does your lifestyle (what you celebrate, worry about, and sacrifice for) suggest about what you trust to secure your future? How confident are you it can truly hold?

PART II

LIVING THE TRUTH

5

A NEW WAY OF SEEING

GOD AT THE CENTER

And he said to him, "You shall love the Lord your God with all your heart and with all your soul and with all your mind. This is the great and first commandment. And a second is like it: You shall love your neighbor as yourself. On these two commandments depend all the Law and the Prophets."

— MATTHEW 22:37–40

Imagine you're a slave at the end of the American Civil War. You've spent years in the cotton fields, being owned, ordered, and overlooked. You don't get to decide where to live, what to eat, or who to marry. Your master makes every choice for you. You've never known freedom.

Then one day, a messenger rides up with good news: "The war is over. You're free."

You blink in disbelief. What does that mean? In one sense, nothing is different. You're still standing in the same dusty field. You still have the same clothes, the same aches, and the same calloused hands.

But in another way, everything has changed. Your legal reality has shifted. Your shackles are gone, and your master has lost his claim to you.

From the outside, it might not look like much is new. But your future now has possibilities. For the first time, you can choose your path and imagine a different life. The world looks the same, but you see it with fresh eyes.

That's what it's like to become a Christian. You're still the same person. But spiritually, everything has changed. You are no longer enslaved to sin. You have a new Master. A new road stretches out in front of you. Your values and desires begin to shift. The way you view yourself, others, and the world takes on a new shape. That shift doesn't happen all at once. It takes time to learn. But it begins the moment you're set free.

We call the way you view the world your worldview.

> A worldview isn't something you think about; it's something you think with.

It's like a pair of contact lenses. You don't notice them once you put them on, but they constantly affect how you see everything else. Let me explain this new worldview with an analogy.

A COPERNICAN SHIFT

Look up at the sky on a clear day. Everything you see suggests the Earth is the center of the universe. The sun rises on one horizon, arcs across the sky, and sets on the other. The moon and stars follow similar patterns. When we stand still, we see the sun move and watch the shadows change. From our perspective, the universe revolves around us.

But study the night sky long enough, and you'll observe something strange. The planets don't always behave the way you'd expect. Their paths wobble, loop, and backtrack. It makes little sense until you realize the problem isn't with the planets; it's with our perspective.

That's what astronomer Nicolaus Copernicus discovered. He realized that the sun, not the earth, is at the center of our galaxy. The Earth isn't the anchor of the solar system. It's just one planet among many, orbiting the sun. His discovery flipped our understanding of the world upside down.

Before we come to faith, we see ourselves in the same way that ancient astronomers saw the world. We believe we're at the center of everything. Life feels like it orbits around us. We measure our actions and weigh our choices by how the results affect us.

From our perspective, God and everyone else are supporting characters in a story where we play the lead. We may not say it out loud, but deep down, we know with every fiber of our being that the world exists for our benefit.

But when saving faith takes hold, it causes a Copernican shift. Suddenly, the story isn't about us anymore. We recognize the truth: God is the center of the universe, and we are not. He doesn't orbit around us. We orbit him. He is the anchor of reality, the source of all life and truth. And we are just one planet among many, held in place by his gravity.

> How we see ourselves in relation to God and other people is one of the most important foundations of a biblical worldview.

If we still believe we're the center, we'll resist God's authority and resent anyone who gets in our way.

But when we accept that God is God, and we are not, it forces us to change how we live. We humble ourselves before God, admitting that he alone defines what is right and good. We stop measuring our worth by comparison and recognize that we're no better than anyone else.

We sin because we think we're more important than anyone else, trampling others to protect our comfort and prioritizing our wants at their expense. But saving faith tells the truth: we are not God and we are neither more nor less important than anyone else.

Once we see God at the center, the two greatest commandments make sense. Jesus summarized the Law and the Prophets with two commands: love God with all our heart, soul, and mind, and love our neighbor as ourselves (Matthew 22:37–40).

That's not random. It flows directly from reality. God is our Creator. He gave us life. He sustains our every breath. Of course, we should love him above everything else.

But what about our neighbors? That's where this new worldview makes a big difference. Knowing that God is at the center means that the rest of us stand side by side as equals. We're all created in his image. We all fall short. And we all matter to him. That's why loving others is central, not optional. It's the natural result of seeing the world the way God does. Let me explain with another analogy.

EQUAL UNDER THE SON

Imagine you're a kid on the playground at school. But instead of joining the kickball game or climbing the jungle gym, you are standing off to the side. You've sized up the other kids racing around and declared them a pack of losers. Their games seem pointless, their jokes aren't funny, and they aren't interested in the right toys. You have decided they're not worth your time.

Then one day, everything changes. An older teenager joins the after-school program. He's smart, funny, kind, and effortlessly confident. Even the teachers laugh at his jokes. You want nothing more than to be his friend.

To your great surprise, he likes you. He seeks you out, listens to you, laughs at your jokes, and treats you like a friend. Your life is now wonderful because you are in the inner circle of the coolest guy around.

Being friends with him changes the entire playground dynamic. Instead of being a loner, you are part of the popular crowd, because he accepts you. Other kids admire you because he calls you his friend.

As great as this newfound admiration is, it also takes some humility. You did nothing to earn this good fortune. It comes from the fact that he welcomes you. But there is another wrinkle.

You're not the only kid he befriends. He also accepts an entire group of those kids you wrote off as losers. Hanging out with him means hanging out with them, because they are also part of his gang.

This cool teenager clearly sees no difference between you and the other kids. He treats them just as he treats you, as equally valuable, lovable, and worthy friends.

Now, you face a decision. How are you going to treat these kids? Are you going to continue thinking you're better than they are? Or will you accept the truth this teenager has shown you: that you are no better and no worse than anyone else on the playground?

He is the sun. In his eyes, you're all planets, equally chosen, equally valued, and held in orbit by the same steady pull of his affection.

Saving faith requires the same worldview shift. When we finally grasp that God is the center, not us, it humbles us. We stop dividing people into "beneath me" or "above me." Instead, we begin to see others the way God sees them, as fellow play-mates, fellow image-bearers, and sinners in need of grace.

That's one reason that Jesus includes loving your neighbor as one of the two greatest commandments. When we refuse, we aren't only breaking a rule; we're denying reality. The self-right-eous stubbornly cling to the lie that they are better, and more deserving than other people. But they fail to realize that whatever standard they use to judge their neighbors unworthy also condemns them. We all fall short of the glory of God and need the same grace and mercy.

Love Is Action

What does it mean to love our neighbors? Are we supposed to feel warm and fuzzy toward everyone we meet? Do we need to treat every person like our best friend? No.

In biblical terms, we recognize love by what it does. Love acts for the good of another person. It doesn't just speak kindly or feel something sincerely. It acts, serves, and gives.

We know God loves us because he acted. He sent his son to save us and bring us eternal life. We know Jesus loves us because his actions proved it. He gave his life for us.

In the same way, we show love in what we do. When saving faith changes our actions, we strive to follow what God says is right and to avoid what God says is wrong. We follow our Lord's example of service. We act for the benefit of others, not because they've earned it, and not because it makes us feel good, but because it's the right thing to do.

That's what love does. Anyone can say the right thing or promise future good deeds, but love is revealed by what it does. Hence the proverb: actions speak louder than words.

But our motivation to love our neighbors is more than being nice. At its core, our motivation is understanding that God is our creator and we are equal before him.

When we trust God to take care of us, we are free to be generous, rather than put ourselves first. When we see our neighbors as equals before God, we are free to love generously without keeping score.

Loving others through our actions isn't an optional upgrade in the Christian life or a bonus feature for especially spiritual people. It results from recognizing that God is the center of the universe.

In his presence, every person stands on equal ground, no matter how we feel about them. We don't show love because it's convenient, it earns us something, or it feels good. We treat others as we would wish to be treated because it reflects our equality before God.

FLIP THE TELESCOPE

This precept of treating others as you want to be treated goes back to the Old Testament. In Leviticus 19:18, God gives both a negative and a positive expression of this command. The positive side is loving your neighbor as yourself. The negative side is avoiding vengeance or holding a grudge.

Vengeance is an external response that retaliates and tries to even the score. Bearing a grudge is an internal response. It nurtures the hurt, refuses to forgive, and encourages resentment to take root.

Both the external and internal responses have the same result; we stay focused on the wrong done to us. The command to love our neighbor flips that perspective. It asks us to stop looking inward and start looking outward.

> Loving our neighbor as ourselves means asking a simple question: If the roles were reversed, how would I want to be treated?

Then do that. When we're the ones in the wrong, we hope for understanding and a chance to make things right. When someone wrongs us, we ought to extend the same patience. We don't need to wait for an apology or demand they make amends first. We act in ways that bring blessings, not hurt, because that's what we'd want if we were in their shoes.

Further, our actions don't depend on how the other person responds. Loving others isn't about getting love in return; it's about recognizing our neighbors matter because God says they do. We show mercy and compassion because every person bears God's image, and we stand as equals before him.

You don't have to be a Christian to act in love. Many people show kindness, generosity, and compassion, regardless of their spiritual beliefs. But Christian love acts in a way that sets it apart. It treats others well, even when they don't treat us well.

As Jesus said, even unbelievers love those who love them back (Luke 6:32–35). But loving someone who wrongs you and showing kindness to someone who hates you is a different kind of love.

That kind of self-sacrificing love marks followers of Jesus because it is rooted in a different worldview. We know we're not the center of the universe. We recognize we are equally guilty, equally in need of rescue, and equally dependent on God's grace.

DIFFERENT ORBITS, EQUAL WORTH

Being equal before God doesn't mean that we all walk the same path in this life. We don't. God does not guarantee everyone equal outcomes. Some people will live with abundance, full of wealth, health, opportunities, and close relationships.

Others will walk a harder road, facing poverty, loneliness, loss, or limitation. Just like characters in a book face distinct challenges, obstacles, and successes, in God's story, our lives look very different.

That doesn't mean God is unfair. It means he gives each of us a different role in the story he's telling. We are not cookie-cutter creatures receiving identical treatment. We are individuals, called to trust him with the life he gives us. Some will carry visible burdens. Others will bear quiet ones. God asks all of us to walk the path he sets before us with faith.

We should not use these differences as an excuse to envy what someone else has. That means learning to be content with the path God has given us, even when it's rocky. It also means striving to avoid comparing, coveting, or complaining because God gave someone else different opportunities and obstacles.

But just as importantly, we're not to use our differences as an excuse to avoid compassion, kindness, and generosity. The command to love our neighbor as ourselves doesn't change based on how little or how much we have. Those with the means to help are called to respond generously when others are in need. Likewise, those in need of help are called to resist resentment or entitlement. Love moves both ways; it gives freely and receives humbly.

SIMPLE BUT HARD

Jesus said, "As you wish that others would do to you, do so to them" (Luke 6:31). We call that the Golden Rule. Notice Jesus does not say, "If you want to be treated well, then treat others well." That might work sometimes, but that's not his point.

Loving your neighbor isn't a strategy for getting what you want; it's a truth about how you're called to live. The Golden Rule reminds us that our needs aren't more urgent, our time isn't more valuable, and our voice is no more important than anyone else's. We are beloved, but we are not above our neighbor. We are walking different roads, but we walk them as equals before the throne of God.

On some level, every human being understands this truth. But it doesn't take long to see how quickly we abandon that principle when it suits us. Sometimes we help ourselves at someone else's expense without even noticing. It can be obvious and destructive, as in cases of stealing, lying, or violence.

But it can also show up in small things like cutting in line, taking the last cookie, ignoring the dirty dishes, forgetting a birthday, or insisting on having our way.

Most of us are empathetic to a point. But then our self-interest kicks in. Just watch a toddler when a parent says no and you'll see what I mean. We don't outgrow selfish behavior so much as we learn how to hide it better. We act as if our behavior is justified because our needs feel urgent, and from our old perspective, they are.

But saving faith replaces that old mindset. Faith teaches us to stop viewing people as obstacles to our happiness or background characters in our personal stories. Instead, we begin to see others as they really are: fellow image-bearers in need of the same grace, patience, and mercy that we ourselves need.

We're not above or beneath them. We stand side by side, equally broken, equally valuable, equally dependent on God's lovingkindness. That perspective doesn't come naturally because we are sinful and selfish. It takes humility, time, and the work of the Holy Spirit. And it takes a deep understanding that love isn't about what others deserve. It's about seeing clearly who God is and who we are.

One of the biggest misunderstandings about Christianity is the idea that Christians think they're better than everyone else. Yet a biblical worldview says otherwise. Thanks to our Copernican shift, we know we are equals before God. Christians don't claim to be better; we claim to be rescued and forgiven.

Every day, life hands us opportunities to apply or ignore this new worldview: a rude comment, a forgotten favor, a friend who doesn't come through, a long line, a short fuse, a conversation that doesn't go our way. Each moment is a chance to choose to show love and to let someone else have their way.

And the truth is, we won't always get it right. In fact, failure will come more often than we'd like. But we'll learn. We are becoming the kind of people who place God at the center of the universe and live by the Golden Rule.

One day, God will make us into people who love like that easily and naturally. But not today, not yet. For now, we live in the tension between who we are and who we are becoming. We shouldn't expect to be like Jesus yet; that's a promise for the life to come.

Next we'll explore Jesus' "new commandment," uncovering how the perspective we've just gained now compels us to a distinctive love for our new family.

SUMMARY

- Becoming a Christian launches a new worldview, comparable to a Copernican revolution: God stands at the universe's center, and everyone orbits around him.
- Loving God and neighbors flows naturally from seeing all people as fellow image-bearers under one sovereign Creator.
- Love is measured by action.
- The Golden Rule ("Treat others as you wish to be treated") is a statement of reality, not a social tactic.
- Christian love stands out because it extends kindness even to enemies, reflecting the believer's recognition that no one stands morally above another.
- Equality before God does not erase life's differences; God calls believers to walk varied paths of abundance or hardship to accomplish his purposes.
- The distinguishing mark of God's children in this age is not flawless performance but a sincere desire and growing resolve to love God and neighbors.

SEE FOR YOURSELF

Philippians 2:5–11; Matthew 7:12–29; Luke 10:25–37;
Matthew 22:23–40.

REFLECTION

When everyday choices put your needs in conflict with
someone else's, what guides your actions? How might that
reveal who (or what) sits at the center of your world?

6

THE CHURCH

FINDING YOUR NEW FAMILY

Whoever says he is in the light and hates his brother is still in darkness. Whoever loves his brother abides in the light, and in him there is no cause for stumbling.

—1 JOHN 2:9–10

Equality before God teaches us a second lesson. Besides loving our neighbors, we show a particular love for fellow believers because we share a spiritual bond. Jesus, Paul, Peter, and John all make this point (Matthew 10:40–42; Ephesians 1:15–16; 1 Peter 1:22–23; 1 John 2:9–11).

Picture a packed stadium on game day. Orange scarves, caps, and even face paint mark everyone who pulls for the home team. As you weave through the crowd, you spot a stranger wrapped in the same blazing orange scarf you're wearing.

Instantly you trade a nod, maybe a quick fist-bump, and shout the team chant together. No introductions are needed because the colors already say you're on the same side.

In the same way, believers welcome anyone whose life shows

they follow Jesus. Our shared allegiance quietly declares that we're in the same family.

There's nothing unusual about loving our relatives. Family loyalty typically comes naturally. But when we choose to associate with people simply because they follow Jesus, that shows that we love Jesus, too. When we love his people, we're honoring him.

THE BADGE OF BELONGING

Jesus made this point when he sent the twelve who became his apostles out to preach the gospel for the first time (Matthew 10). Before they left, he gave them a sobering warning: this trip will not be a victory tour.

The gospel divides. It calls on people to choose, and that choice can fracture even the closest human relationships. Then he said something striking: "Whoever receives you receives me, and whoever receives me receives him who sent me" (Matthew 10:40–42).

To "receive" someone is to welcome them, to accept them and say, "You're one of mine." When people embraced the apostles, it demonstrated they belonged to the one who sent them.

Then Jesus broadened the point: welcoming any ordinary follower of Jesus shows hospitality to their Lord. Even a simple kindness such as giving a disciple a cup of cold water shows you love Jesus.

Following Jesus does not require grand gestures. It is revealed in treating fellow disciples as family. We can guess a person's relationship with God by how they respond to his people. If you view other people as kindred spirits because they love Jesus, you reveal your own love for him. If you mock or ridicule them for that same devotion, your attitude tells a different story.

SPIRITUAL SIBLINGS

When Jesus gives what he calls a "new commandment," he is not introducing the idea of loving your neighbor for the first time. The call to love your neighbor goes back to Leviticus. What's new is the emphasis he places on how his disciples love each other.

He says:

> A new commandment I give to you, that you love one another: just as I have loved you, you also are to love one another. By this all people will know that you are my disciples, if you have love for one another (John 13:34–35).

The world doesn't recognize us as disciples of Jesus because we're nice, agreeable, or full of spiritual karma. Jesus said people will know who we follow by watching how we treat other followers of Jesus. We won't persecute, mock, or ridicule them. We'll see them as family.

Believers may come from different races, backgrounds, social classes, or personalities. We may not vote, dress, or think the same. But if we're both seeking God, if we both love Jesus and trust in his word, we recognize each other. We're not merely acquaintances who believe the same doctrine. We're brothers and sisters in Christ.

Loving our fellow believers isn't about personal preference. It's about spiritual identity. We belong to Jesus, which means we belong to each other. The love we show other believers isn't fake or forced. It comes from knowing we're on the same journey, pursuing the same Messiah, depending on the same grace, and destined to spend eternity together.

Jesus makes this point again in a different context. He describes the final judgment when he will separate his people

61

from the rest, like a shepherd separates his sheep from goats. What marks his people as his? It is not their church attendance or theological brilliance; it is their love for his people.

Jesus said:

> For I was hungry and you gave me food, I was thirsty and you gave me drink, I was a stranger and you welcomed me, I was naked and you clothed me, I was sick and you visited me, I was in prison and you came to me (Matthew 25:31–36)

His listeners were confused. They asked, "Lord, when did we do those things for you?"

Jesus answered, "Truly, I say to you, as you did it to one of the least of these my brothers, you did it to me" (Matthew 25:40).

When we care for another believer, we're not just being polite. We are revealing our love for Jesus. "Seeing Christ" in someone doesn't mean we think they're flawless. It means we recognize a fellow traveler who loves the same Lord, leans on the same grace, and is headed toward the same eternal home. That shared identity turns ordinary acts like offering a meal, a visit, or a listening ear into quiet declarations that we belong to Jesus.

FAITH YOU CAN SEE

The apostle Paul makes this connection plain in Ephesians 1. He writes:

> Because I have heard of your faith in the Lord Jesus and your love toward all the saints, I do not cease to give thanks for you (Ephesians 1:15–16).

Notice what he praises: their faith in Jesus as evidenced by their love for other believers. Paul knows their faith is real because he has heard how they treat God's people.

Faith is invisible. It doesn't leave a mark on our skin or change the shape of our face. But it absolutely changes how we treat one another. When we belong to Jesus, we begin to love like Jesus. And one of the clearest ways that love shows up is in how we care for other believers.

Of course, not everyone who claims to follow Jesus actually does. Scripture warns us that false teachers and counterfeit faith will exist side by side with the real thing.

How do we know who truly belongs to Christ? Jesus said we'll know his followers by their actions. We'll see a difference in their values, choices, and goals. Over time it should become evident that they are seeking God.

Another test is how they treat other believers. If someone mocks or belittles Christians for taking their faith seriously, that reveals where they stand. Ridiculing the faithful is not a mark of discipleship. It's a mark of resistance.

Loving Jesus means loving his people.

The bond between believers isn't just friendship. It's family. And that connection flows from the most foundational truth in Scripture: God is real. He created us. He is at the center, not us. We all fall short. We all need grace, and we all find it at the same cross.

So when we see others who believe that same gospel, who walk in the same direction, we recognize them as family. It shows up in how we treat them, in patience, support, forgiveness, and joy. That kind of love isn't theoretical. It's real, and it's one of the clearest ways the world sees who Jesus is.

So how do we live that kind of life? That's the question we'll take up next.

Summary

- Scripture teaches that while Christians are to love all neighbors, they owe a special, family-like affection to fellow believers because a spiritual bond unites them in Christ.
- Welcoming or serving a disciple of Jesus shows we welcome and honor Christ.
- Jesus' "new commandment" elevates mutual love among disciples as a distinguishing mark by which the world will recognize followers of Jesus.
- True allegiance to Jesus therefore transcends earthly divisions of race, class, politics, or personality, forming a new, eternal household in which believers treat one another as family.
- Conversely, mocking or persecuting earnest Christians marks a heart in spiritual darkness.
- Loving fellow Christians is not optional sentimentality; it is an unmistakable hallmark of saving faith.

See for Yourself

Matthew 10:40–43; John 13:1–20; Galatians 5:25–6:5; 1 John 3:13–24.

Reflection

Observe a community you belong to or are exploring. How does the way its members care for one another confirm or contradict the values they profess? What can you learn from that?

7

DAILY LIFE

WHAT FOLLOWING JESUS LOOKS LIKE

If you confess with your mouth that Jesus is Lord and believe in your heart that God raised him from the dead, you will be saved.

— ROMANS 10:9

Maybe you've recently decided to follow Jesus. Or maybe you're still curious but not yet convinced. Either way, hopefully you caught a glimpse of something compelling in the gospel and you want to know what comes next.

What would it look like to orient your life around Jesus? Does it mean selling everything and heading to the mission field? Are you supposed to swap your weekend plans for silent retreats and nonstop prayer? Should you stand on a street corner and tell people about Jesus?

For some, God may call them to a life that looks radically different from their pre-Christian life. But for most of us, following Jesus doesn't mean a change in career. It means a change in perspective. We may still go to the same job or care for the same people, but we do it with a new set of goals and attitudes.

Though each of us will follow very different life paths, broadly speaking, we have the same three goals for our journey:

Say it: Confess Jesus is Lord.
Mean it: Fear God.
Keep it: Persevere in faith.

These three goals aren't extra, optional upgrades. They define what it means to live as a believer. These goals shape our discipleship and are part of whatever life God calls us to walk.

SAY IT: CONFESS JESUS IS LORD

> Therefore I make known to you that no one speaking by the Spirit of God says, "Jesus is accursed," and no one can say, "Jesus is Lord," except by the Holy Spirit.
>
> — 1 CORINTHIANS 12:3

What does being a Christian look like? The apostle Paul answered this question for the Corinthians.

Imagine a man named Marcus, a Gentile living in ancient Corinth. Before he met Jesus, Marcus worshiped at a pagan temple where spiritual experience meant drinking wine, inhaling incense, and working himself into an emotional, trance-like state.

But then Marcus heard a traveling evangelist named Paul preach the gospel of Jesus Christ. Now Marcus is a Christian, worshiping a Jewish Messiah.

He assumes that his new spirituality will still look and feel the same as his old idol worship. He expects it to be mystical and emotional, maybe even dramatic.

Some of his new Christian friends agree. They tell Marcus that genuine faith is marked by speaking in tongues (a supernatural gift where someone speaks a language they don't know). Since Marcus hasn't had that experience, they suggest that he's not really saved.

But others in his church disagree. They believe salvation is about trusting Jesus, and speaking in tongues is irrelevant. As the debate grows, the church starts taking sides. The tongue-speakers look down on everyone else.

Marcus begins to doubt his faith: *Do I really belong? Am I missing something?*

Eventually, someone writes to Paul for help. In response, Paul cuts through the confusion with a single, powerful sentence: No one can say Jesus is Lord unless he has the Holy Spirit (1 Corinthians 12:3).

The mark of a believer isn't a flashy, supernatural experience like speaking in tongues.

The mark of a believer is what you believe about Jesus.

CONFESSION IS THE LINE IN THE SAND

Saving faith means taking a side. When confronted with the claims of Christ, we have only two options: accept or reject him. Paul says that those who say and mean, "Jesus is Lord," are genuine believers. In a sense, the Spirit takes control of your mouth and your life, but not to speak in tongues, to confess that Jesus is Lord.

Paul makes the same point in Romans 10:9: "If you confess with your mouth that Jesus is Lord and believe in your heart that God raised him from the dead, you will be saved."

Peter preached the same message in Acts 2:36: "God has made this Jesus, whom you crucified, both Lord and Christ."

In his advice to the Corinthians, Paul includes both the positive (Jesus is Lord) and the negative (Jesus is accursed). For the Corinthians, this conviction was a unique feature of the Christian faith. In their pagan trances, people could say anything, sometimes even contradicting themselves.

But in Christianity, truth matters. You can't believe both that Jesus is Lord and not Lord at the same time.

TRUTH OVER EXPERIENCE

The phrase "Jesus is Lord" is not religious filler. It summarizes the gospel. It means we believe Jesus has the authority to forgive sins and the power to grant eternal life. It means that we follow his teaching as truth and his commands as the path for our lives. He is the one we worship, the one we obey, and the one we trust above all.

Teaching us the truth is how the Spirit works. The Spirit doesn't simply produce emotion or supernatural experiences. The Spirit leads us to see and understand the truth of the gospel. If someone rejects Jesus, mocks him, or consistently ignores his words, they do not have the Spirit, no matter how spiritual or religious they may seem.

TRUE SPIRITUALITY

Today, people use the word spiritual in all kinds of ways. Some say that it means feeling deeply connected to the universe. Others associate it with simplicity, self-denial, helping the poor, or living for a noble cause. Still others think being spiritual means doing "big things" for God like becoming a missionary or giving everything to the poor.

But Paul would say being spiritual isn't about your job, emotions, or experiences. It's not about status, performance, avoiding material things, or having a dramatic backstory. A Christian who works in an office, raises kids, or stocks shelves at a store is no less spiritual than someone preaching the gospel in a remote jungle village. Why? Because true spirituality is not defined by how you serve God or by what you feel. It's defined by what you believe about Jesus.

Becoming a spiritual person involves a specific worldview shift. It's not measured by how inspired you feel after worship, how generous you are, or how devoted you appear. It's not even about being a nice person.

The dividing line is this: Do you believe that Jesus is Lord in a way that changes your life? That confession is the most important declaration any person can make.

~

MEAN IT: FEAR GOD

The fear of the LORD is the beginning of knowledge;
fools despise wisdom and instruction.

— PROVERBS 1:7

After confessing Jesus is Lord, the next goal is to fear God more than anything else. That idea can sound strange at first. Doesn't the Bible tell us not to be afraid? Isn't God loving and kind? He is.

But the Bible also teaches that fearing God is the beginning of wisdom. But this fear is not a fear that drives us away from him. It's a fear that puts him in his rightful place. Fear is a powerful motivator. It drives our decisions, often without us realizing it.

Imagine you detest public speaking. You'd do almost anything to avoid giving a speech. But then your boss gives you an ultimatum: "Give this presentation or you're fired."

Now you're forced to choose. Which fear carries more weight? If you fear your boss more than the audience, you'll speak. If you fear public speaking more than your boss, you'll refuse to give the speech. Either way, what you fear most determines what you do.

> Fearing God means letting what he says weigh more than anything else.

When you face a choice, his opinion matters most. That's what the Bible means when it says the fear of the Lord is the beginning of wisdom. It's the starting line for clear thinking and right action. It's not fear that makes you hide. It's fear that makes you choose what God says is right. But we can go wrong in that fear two ways.

How to Fear the King

Imagine that you live in a kingdom ruled by a great and powerful king. This king is someone you've heard about but never met. One day, a friend invites you to his home.

You casually shrug and say, "Maybe I will come. Maybe I won't. Let me see how my day is going."

But when that same invitation comes from the king himself, you treat it differently. There's no hesitation. You drop everything, clear your schedule, and leave early to make sure you arrive on time. The king is not your buddy. He holds the power to bless you or ruin your life. His favor matters in ways that nothing else does.

When you arrive at the palace, you discover something unexpected. The king is not only powerful; he is also kind and generous. He asks thoughtful questions about how he can help your business, your town, and your family. He is fair and extremely wise.

You leave the meeting with a new understanding of who he is and the role he plays in your life. And that's where you can go wrong. Because from that point onward, two temptations pull in opposite directions.

On one side, you might grow complacent. The king was kind, after all. Maybe you think of him as a buddy. You might take his kindness for granted, assuming he's a pushover because he's nice.

Next time he calls, you show up late or not at all, assuming he'll understand. You ignore his rules, convinced he'll let it slide, because you and the king are pals.

That's what it looks like to lose your fear of him. You forget that his kindness flows from strength, not weakness, and you stop taking him seriously.

On the other side, you might become so overwhelmed by his power that you forget his grace. Obsessing over every detail, you start to fear slipping up and losing his favor. Avoidance sets in, not because you doubt his authority, but because his compassion fades from view.

The result? Living in terror instead of a healthy kind of fear. One mistake feels like the end. That's what it looks like to forget his grace and kindness.

Both responses (treating him too casually or avoiding him in dread) miss the mark. And we can make the same mistakes with God. We can treat God too lightly, as if he exists only to bless us and make our lives easier. Or we can live in fear of his judgment, unsure if he really loves us.

But the fear of the Lord, the kind Scripture calls the beginning of wisdom, holds both truths together. God is the ultimate authority. He is holy and just, and he will hold us accountable.

But he is also merciful, patient, and kind. When we fear God rightly, we don't run from him; we run to him. We take him seriously because we trust his character.

A MATTER OF BELIEF

When sending the twelve people who would become his apostles out to preach, Jesus warned them about what they would face. He predicted people would hate them because they hate Jesus (Matthew 10:24–28). Some would even try to kill them.

In that situation, Jesus warned his disciples to fear God more than the crowds. He encouraged them not to let fear of others stop them from doing what God called them to do. Jesus said:

> And do not fear those who kill the body but cannot kill the soul. Rather fear him who can destroy both soul and body in hell (Matthew 10:28).

When you're trying to decide how to act, your motivating factor should be how God will react, not your peers, even if your peers can kill your body.

Ultimately, who we fear is a question of belief. In Matthew 10, Jesus was sending his disciples on a journey where they could get jailed and beaten. Why would they go? Why would anyone keep walking to the next town after being beaten in the last one?

Because they believed that God was worth following. They feared him more than they feared anything else.

That kind of fear isn't anxiety; it's allegiance. It's about knowing who holds ultimate authority and choosing to follow him, no matter what. When we fear God rightly, it does not paralyze us. It anchors us. It becomes the steady foundation under our feet. Even when the ground around us shifts, we know where to stand.

Staying Awake

The Bible describes this focus on fearing God as staying awake, being sober and alert. It's hard to stay focused when we distract ourselves with busywork and entertainment. We get so caught up in the noise of daily life that we forget that the gospel matters. We forget that the biggest problem we face is not fame, fortune, health, wealth, or building our resume. The most important question we face is: Do we fear God?

The gospel cuts deep into our lives. It makes a difference in every moment of every day. We need to remember who we are dealing with. Jesus Christ is not our buddy who is there if we need him and leaves us alone when we don't. He is the Lord of Lords and the King of Kings, who holds the gift of eternal life in his hands.

The one person in the universe we must come to terms with is Jesus. There is a proper sense in which we should fear him. But we balance that fear with the knowledge that he is also a generous, merciful, and compassionate king.

Today we may face troubles, but those troubles all raise the same question: *Who do I fear most?* Maybe you'll be persecuted, mocked, or evicted. Maybe you'll lose a promotion or a friend. What's most important? Avoiding those troubles or following God?

Everyone faces these questions: *What is my life going to be about? What am I going to believe so strongly that it changes the way I live?* Jesus offers the clearest path forward; fear God first, and everything else will be in proper perspective.

KEEP IT: PERSEVERE IN FAITH

Be strong in the Lord and in the strength of his might. Put on the whole armor of God, that you may be able to stand against the schemes of the devil.

— EPHESIANS 6:10–11

After confessing that Jesus is Lord and learning to fear God, the last goal is to persevere in faith no matter what. Your lifelong mission is to stick with Jesus to the end.

As a new believer, I thought faith was the act of belief at the moment of conversion. I pictured it as throwing a switch. One moment, I rejected the gospel. Then I flipped the switch by praying a sinner's prayer.

Now that I had faith, I assumed I never had to think about faith again, and that my goal was to learn to be a better Christian and a nicer person.

But faith is not a one-time event. Faith is a new set of beliefs that changes the way we understand the world every moment of every day. Faith weaves itself into the fabric of our worldview, so that we see the world the way God sees it. Believing the gospel means that we hold to the four convictions of R.E.A.L. faith and strive to live each day in light of those convictions.

STAND FIRM

Paul describes the Christian life as a battle, not with other people, but with unseen spiritual forces working to pull us away from Jesus. In Ephesians 6, he says we're in a war.

But the war is not about changing the world or scoring victories for Jesus in the public square. The battle is much more personal. It's about clinging to Jesus, no matter what.

Paul's rallying cry is simple: Stand firm (Ephesians 6:10–13).

Standing firm means holding your ground in faith.

It means refusing to be pushed off course, even when everything around you feels like it's trying to pull you away from God. We don't muscle through using our own strength. We stand on the promises of the gospel, trusting that they are true and that God will not let us go. Even if every force of darkness lines up against us, we don't move.

This is not a pretend battle or a side issue. We are in a fight with the powers of evil for our very souls. Satan doesn't show up with pitchforks and fanfare. Instead, he usually hits us with lies, temptations, and distractions, anything to pull us away from the truth.

And we can't opt out or ignore it. Paul isn't saying, "Now that you've secured your spot in heaven, go take a few swings at the devil in the marketplace."

He's saying you are in a battle over your faith. The danger isn't out there somewhere. It's right here: Will you keep trusting Jesus? Or will you give up and walk away?

To stand firm, Paul encourages us to put on the armor of God, not actual armor, of course, but spiritual preparation. That means anchoring ourselves in the truth and remembering the gospel. It means striving to live out our faith, even when it's hard, and trusting God's promises while clinging to the hope of salvation. Most importantly, it means relying on the Spirit of God, who teaches us what is true and reminds us when we're tempted to forget.

At the center of the battle is the question: Will we keep our eyes on what's true? That's the challenge. Will we keep trusting God, even when the world pulls us in the opposite direction? Or will we drift with the crowd and follow the path of least resistance?

Picture the battle as crossing a rushing river on a narrow bridge. The water is loud and wild. The current pulls at everything in its path. But the bridge is secure. As long as you keep your eyes forward and your feet on the planks, you'll make it across.

The danger comes when you get distracted, when you stop walking, dip your toes in the swirling water, or start doubting whether the bridge will hold.

The gospel is that bridge. The hope of salvation keeps us steady. You don't have to fight the current. You just have to keep walking, one step at a time, trusting that God will get you to the other side.

THE DANGER OF SLEEP

Too often, we lose sight of the battle. Life distracts us. The pressures and responsibilities of the day lull us into a kind of spiritual sleep. We think that our biggest problems are the cares of this world like getting a new job, saving more money, or winning that ongoing family argument.

How we handle those things matters, but they're not the main issue. They can pull our focus down to the surface of life, so that we forget the bigger picture. We forget about God.

Behind every hardship, there's a deeper reality. All the suffering and stress we face is part of a much larger story: the battle for our souls and the maturing of our faith. That pressure tempts us to give up on God, to reach for quick fixes, to trade away what's eternal for what's easy right now. And that's exactly what the enemy wants. We'll talk more about that in the next chapter.

THIEF IN THE NIGHT

Both Paul and Jesus warned that the return of Christ will be unexpected, like a thief in the night (1 Thessalonians 5:1–11; Luke 12:35–40). What makes a thief dangerous is surprise. You go to bed assuming tomorrow will be just like today.

But while you're asleep, the thief breaks in and takes everything of value. If you'd known he was coming, you would have locked the doors and stayed alert. That's the nature of a thief. He counts on catching you off guard.

For those who don't believe, that's what the return of Christ will be like. Life will feel normal until suddenly everything changes. But for believers, it's different. We may not know the day or the hour that Jesus will return, but we know that he's coming. We live with open eyes and prepared hearts.

We're not surprised, because we've already taken shelter in his mercy. We've already repented and received his forgiveness. When he comes, we won't be scrambling to make things right. We'll be standing on grace. For us, his return isn't like a thief in the night. It's more like a long-expected friend finally arriving.

Meanwhile, the world sleeps. Paul says that they use the night to get drunk and sleep, wasting their lives while ignoring the waterfall ahead. But believers live in the light of day. We're awake. Because we believe the gospel, we repent, and we wait eagerly for Christ to return. While others drift through life unaware, we stay sober and alert. Our minds are clear. We see what's true.

> The central challenge and calling of the Christian life is
> to stand firm in saving faith.

That kind of faith doesn't spring up fully formed overnight. It starts small, maybe with a simple prayer or a flicker of understanding. But as the Spirit teaches us, our faith grows. It becomes vibrant, mature, and real. Over time, we learn what it means to trust God, not just in theory, but in the middle of life's mess.

With our priorities now centered on Jesus, we're ready to face the bumps and bruises of real life.

Next, we'll discover how the same gospel that sets our course also supplies a quiet resilience that keeps us moving forward when the road gets rough.

SUMMARY

Three non-negotiable goals define a believer's life:

- Say it: Confess Jesus is Lord.
- Mean it: Fear God.
- Keep it: Persevere in faith.

- Confessing "Jesus is Lord" is the decisive line in the sand: the Spirit-empowered declaration that distinguishes genuine Christian faith from merely emotional or mystical religious experiences.
- Fearing God means letting his values outweigh every competing pressure, neither presuming on his kindness nor cowering in terror, but holding his majesty and mercy together.
- Perseverance is a lifelong combat to stand firm on gospel promises.
- Scripture urges believers to stay awake, sober, and alert because Christ's return will be sudden for the unprepared.

SEE FOR YOURSELF

1 Corinthians 12:1–3; 1 Peter 5:6–14; Ephesians 6:10–24;
Proverbs 1:7–9.

REFLECTION

Who or what do you recognize (consciously or unconsciously)
as the highest authority in your life? How is that allegiance
shaping your everyday decisions and long-term direction?

8

TRIALS

HOW GOD USES HARD TIMES

Count it all joy, my brothers, when you meet trials of various kinds, for you know that the testing of your faith produces steadfastness. And let steadfastness have its full effect, that you may be perfect and complete, lacking in nothing.

— JAMES 1:2–4

We love stories that end well. From fairy tales to feel-good movies, we're drawn to the promise of "happily ever after." And sometimes without realizing it, we bring that expectation into our faith. We assume trusting God will shield us from hardship and trusting Jesus means our lives will be smoother. But Scripture tells a different story. The promised happy ending arrives in the kingdom of heaven.

The Bible never promises an easy path in this earthly life. In fact, it promises the opposite. Trials are not interruptions to the plan. They are part of the plan. Jesus, James, Peter, and Paul all make that point (John 15:17–21; James 1:1–5; 1 Peter 1:6–7; Romans 5:3–5).

Difficulties aren't proof that something's gone wrong, or that God is mad at us. They're often the very means that God uses to grow us, stretch us, and deepen our faith.

A trial is anything that tests your trust in God.

It might be something big like a tragedy, illness, or financial loss. Or it might be something less obvious but just as real, like ongoing loneliness, a strained relationship, frustration, or disappointment. While trials come in all shapes and sizes, they invite the same question: *Will I keep trusting God?*

James urges us to "count it all joy" when we meet trials, not because the struggle feels good, but because we know what God is doing through it (James 1:2–4). Trials test our faith. And tested faith produces perseverance, that spiritual resilience that keeps us rooted when life shakes us.

Over time, that kind of faith leads to maturity, not maturity in the sense of perfection, but completeness and wholeness, a kind of spiritual muscle that equips us to endure, trust, and love well. That's God's goal: not a fairy tale ending, but a mature faith that leads to a transformed life.

REFINED LIKE GOLD

Picture an ancient goldsmith at work in his shop, patiently tending a small fire. In his hands is a lump of raw gold. It's dull, mixed with impurities, and easy to overlook. To most people, it looks like a worthless rock. But the goldsmith knows better. He sees what it can become.

He places the gold into the fire, adjusting the heat with precision. As the metal melts, the impurities rise to the surface and burn away. The longer it stays in the flame, the purer it becomes.

But it's a delicate process. Remove it from the flames too

soon, and the impurities remain. The goldsmith watches closely, knowing exactly how much heat is needed for how long to achieve perfect refinement.

Peter tells us that God uses trials the same way in our lives (1 Peter 1:7). Trials are the fire he uses to refine our faith. They burn away what's weak and false, our doubts, our selfishness, our illusions of control, and leave behind something stronger, purer, and more real.

It's not an easy process. Sometimes it hurts. Sometimes it feels like we're being pushed past our limits. But the Master Goldsmith never takes his eyes off us. He knows exactly what we need.

When the refining is done, what remains is more valuable than gold. Gold may be precious in this life, but it doesn't last. Gold won't survive the fire of final judgment, but a faith that endures trials will. A tested, steadfast faith results in something eternal: an inheritance in heaven that can never spoil, fade, or be taken away.

That's why genuine faith matters so much. Mature faith is more than believing the right things. It's about learning to trust God through the fire. Trials reveal whether our faith is built on convenience or conviction.

And when we come through the other side of a trial still holding on to our faith, we know our faith is real. Because saving faith is worth more than all the gold in the world, God ensures our faith grows, one trial at a time.

Pressure Tests the Metal

You'd be hard-pressed to find a part of the New Testament that doesn't talk about trials. Over and over, Scripture emphasizes that one of God's main purposes in this life is to take us through difficult situations, not to crush our faith, but to prove it. And in the proving, to strengthen it.

How is faith proved? It holds. When pressure comes, it doesn't collapse. Trials bring choices that expose where we stand. They force us to ask questions like: *Will I stay faithful to my spouse when temptation offers a quick escape? Will I tell the truth on a job application, even if a lie would help me get ahead? Will I stand up for what's right when it costs me something, maybe a friendship, a reputation, or a promotion?*

These hardships reveal what we really trust. They aren't random. They're part of God's agenda to grow us into people who not only profess faith, but live it.

Trials don't test whether we're good enough for heaven. That verdict is already in: we're sinful by nature, unable to fix ourselves. Without the grace of God and the blood of Christ, we have no hope at all. None of us is worthy of salvation. That's why grace is a gift.

So what is being tested? Not the worthiness of our characters, but the authenticity of our faith. Trials force us to face the doubts we all wrestle with: *How do I know my faith is genuine? What if I give up one day? Does God really love and forgive me?*

Jesus, James, Paul, and Peter all point to the same answer: when you endure a trial and keep trusting God, that endurance becomes proof, not for God, who already knows your heart, but for you. It gives you something solid to stand on.

You can look back and say, "Yes, that was hard. But my faith held. God kept me. I'm still standing." That kind of experience deepens confidence. It gives you tangible, physical evidence that all the promises of God belong to you.

And trials don't just prove faith, they grow it. Through hardship, we gain wisdom. We begin to see life differently. We become more mature, grounded, and aware of what truly matters. Trials are one of God's primary tools for shaping us into people who live wisely and belong fully to him.

STRONGER ON A NEW FIELD

Let me give you an example. Imagine you're on a professional soccer team. You've trained hard and earned your starting spot. The season is going well, even though some of your wins have been a little too close for comfort. You're proud of the team's success, and the season is on track.

One day after practice, a teammate pulls you aside. "Coach has been bribing the referees to throw games our way," he says.

You laugh until he shows you a paper trail that proves it is true. You're shocked and disappointed. Reluctantly, you admit your friend is right.

But the next day, you show up to practice like normal, acting as if nothing has changed. After all, what else can you do?

Weeks go by, and then God turns up the heat. The league opens an investigation. At a public meeting, the coach denies everything. He's slick, confident, and convincing.

"There's no proof," he says, answering each accusation like he's done this before.

But then your teammate stands up. Quietly but clearly, he says, "Coach is lying. I have proof." As he lays out the evidence, Coach doesn't flinch.

"He just made all that evidence up," the coach says. He looks your friend in the eye and says, "Can you prove that evidence existed before today? Has anyone else ever seen it?"

Your teammate looks at you. Now it's real. You've said you believe your friend. Now you must live like it. Suddenly it's not just his word against the coach's; it's yours too.

You could continue staying silent, hoping to keep your place on a winning team. Or you could speak up and risk everything.

Until this moment, your belief was genuine, but untested. Now the test forces it into the open.

You stand up and say in a steady voice, "He's telling the truth. I saw the evidence last month."

Sadly, the league prefers a cover-up to a public scandal. They quietly release the coach and a couple of referees. They trade you and your teammate to new teams, maybe as payback, maybe not.

But next season, under a new coach and with new challenges, you are different. You're stronger. Wiser. You've learned that God is in control in ways that aren't always obvious. And your new teammates see it. They respect you, not because you're the most talented player on the field, but because they know you're someone they can count on to tell the truth.

Maturity doesn't mean perfect obedience. And wisdom doesn't mean we never fail. In fact, one mark of wisdom is being able to see our own sin more clearly. As we grow in faith, we become quicker to repent. We're slower to justify our actions. Our old excuses sound hollow. A quiet humility settles in.

Maturity isn't the same as being tough, either. God isn't testing our courage. He's testing our faith. Wisdom doesn't mean that we breeze through tragedy without blinking. It means we've found an anchor that holds, even when life shakes us. It means we've learned to hold more loosely to the things of this world and to face hardship with a growing sense of confidence and hope.

It's important to remember what God has and has not promised. He hasn't promised ease, comfort, or prosperity. But he has promised to shape us into people who reflect his character, people who are mature, and ready for the life to come.

Trials may bring deep pain, but they also carry an important purpose. They take us where we truly want to go. They test and mature our faith, and faith opens the door to the kingdom of heaven.

FINDING JOY IN THE FURNACE

Scripture often talks about joy while suffering. That can sound confusing, maybe even unrealistic. But joy isn't about pretending everything is fine.

> Joy is the natural response we have when we know
> something good is on the way.

So why would trials lead to joy? When we truly embrace the hope of the gospel, we start focusing more on the result of the trial than the difficulty of it.

Rejoicing during suffering isn't denial. It's clarity. It's the steady, confident assurance that this hardship has a purpose, and that purpose is worth it.

As our faith matures, we learn to rejoice, not because life gets easier, but because our hope becomes more certain. We know we will inherit eternal life, not because we've earned it, but because Jesus secured it for us.

If we have that promise, we have everything worth having. Without it, even an easy life can leave us empty. Joy flows from knowing that our eternal future is secure, even if today might be hard.

That doesn't mean that we have to feel happy when suffering strikes. We may grieve. We may feel weary, afraid, or overwhelmed.

But even then, we can rejoice in what God has done for us through Christ. We can hold on to the bigger picture. Our trials are real, but they're not final. In light of eternity, they're temporary. Struggling may last for a season, but salvation lasts forever.

When trials come, our first instinct is usually to ask God to change our circumstances. We want the pressure removed and the hardship lifted. That's natural.

But Scripture shifts our perspective. It teaches us that the most important question isn't "When will this trial end?" but rather "How will I respond to God in the midst of it?"

God loves us too much to change our current circumstances without also changing our hearts. That's why trials matter. They're not roadblocks. They're opportunities to grow in faith, endurance, and trust.

When we understand what's at stake and what we stand to gain, we can rejoice, even in the fire of our troubles, because what God is producing in us is far more valuable than anything we're giving up. We don't rejoice because we suffer, but because of where suffering takes us.

Many people assume, *If God really loved me, life would be easy.* But that's not how love works, not with God, and not even with people. Good parents don't remove every challenge. They guide, correct, and prepare their child through the difficulties of life. God does the same.

His goal isn't to make us comfortable. It's to make us people of faith. Scripture never says that believers will be spared from pain. It says the opposite: we'll face trials, but not alone. Trials don't mean that God is distant or angry. Often, they're proof he's near and actively at work, shaping us into people with strong, mature faith.

GRACE RESTORES

What if, in an important moment of testing, you stumble? Consider the apostle Peter. Jesus once told his disciples:

> If you acknowledge me before others, I will acknowledge you before my Father in heaven. But if you deny me before others, I will also deny you (Matthew 10:32–33).

It's a sobering warning. If we reject Jesus, he will reject us.

But the reverse is also true. If we remain faithful to him, he will stand with us.

In one of the most critical moments of Jesus' life, Peter denied him (Luke 22:54–62). Judas betrayed Jesus, leading the authorities to him. They arrested Jesus and brought him before the Jewish court. The road to the cross had begun.

If ever there was a moment to stand firm, this was it. But instead of showing courage, Peter caved. Just as Jesus had predicted, Peter swore three times that he didn't even know Jesus.

Peter did exactly what Jesus warned against. He denied his Lord. And yet, Jesus didn't cast him aside. After the resurrection, Jesus sought Peter out. Jesus restored him, forgave him, and entrusted him with a mission: "Feed my sheep" (John 21:15–19). The same man who once denied Jesus carried the gospel message boldly into the world.

Peter's denial was real. It revealed his fear and weakness in that moment. But it wasn't the end of his story. Over time, Peter grew into a man of deep conviction and faith. Church history tells us that he was eventually imprisoned, beaten, and martyred. He refused to deny Jesus again, even at the cost of his life.

When Jesus uses strong, black-and-white language, like "deny me and I will deny you," he's not laying down a one-strike-and-you-are-out policy. He often speaks in bold terms to make us stop and think about his point.

That doesn't mean that there's no room for failure or forgiveness. Like Peter, every believer stumbles. None of us follows Jesus perfectly or consistently. Sometimes we act with courage. Other times we fall short.

What matters is the direction of your life. Do you keep coming back to Jesus? Do you keep trusting, repenting, and growing?

Peter's story reminds us that a failure is not final. Even in our lowest moments, God is still at work. Ultimately, saving faith endures. It may falter, but it does not disappear. And over time, our lives will bear witness to our faith.

The War We Win

Right now, we're in a war, and the enemy is sin. We see its damage and feel its weight. Trials remind us that the battle is real and ongoing.

But we also know how this battle ends. Jesus has already won. The cross proves God will one day free us completely from sin and death. Every sorrow, every hardship, every tear will be wiped away for good. That hope gives us a reason to rejoice in the middle of the struggle.

Our trials aren't meaningless or random. They have a purpose. Through them, God refines our faith, reminds us we belong to Jesus, and directs our hope toward what truly lasts: the promise of eternal life. But knowing that God uses trials to teach us still leaves a practical question hanging in the air: How do we face them? We'll tackle that in the next section.

Summary

- Trials are part of God's plan, not detours.
- Trials prove that our faith is genuine. When we endure and continue to trust God, we gain assurance that our faith is real.
- Joy in trials comes from perspective, not ease. We rejoice because we know what suffering produces and promises.
- Faith doesn't mean that we never stumble. Like Peter, we may fail in moments of fear or weakness, but God's grace restores and strengthens us.

- Maturity isn't perfection or toughness. It's humility, repentance, and growing confidence in God's faithfulness.

SEE FOR YOURSELF

1 Peter 1:1–13; James 1:1–8; Isaiah 43:1–3; Hebrews 12:5–11.

REFLECTION

Think about a time when you faced a hard trial. What did you learn from it?

PART III

CONFRONTING THE LIES

9

HOLINESS

LEARNING TO DESIRE WHAT'S GOOD

Incline my heart to your testimonies, and not to selfish gain! Turn my eyes from looking at worthless things; and give me life in your ways.

— PSALM 119:36–37

The toughest temptations, the stickiest obstacles, and the hardest choices all share one common thread: desire. Whether we're talking about lingering over a questionable website, lying to gain the fast track at work, or wondering if one more swipe of the credit card really matters, we're facing a choice of priorities. The temptation may be for comfort, connection, control, or pleasure, but it always whispers the same question: *What matters more to me, what I want or what God wants?*

When Paul wrote to correct the young church in Thessalonica, he started with encouragement. They had embraced the gospel with joy, even in the face of hardship. As a whole, they were doing well. But the Thessalonians struggled in two areas:

sex and work. In short, Paul tells them to get a job and stop sleeping around (1 Thessalonians 4:1–12).

He begins his advice to the Thessalonians with a simple but weighty statement:

"This is the will of God, your sanctification: that you abstain from sexual immorality" (1 Thessalonians 4:3).

Most of us skip past that first phrase ("This is the will of God, your sanctification") and jump to what looks like the headline: "Abstain from sexual immorality."

Yet that first line is the foundation on which Paul's advice depends. It does more than introduce the topic; it tells us the destination God has in view. When we grasp that framework, we see that Paul's call to sexual purity isn't a random rule but a crucial piece of God's larger project.

God's will is that we become sanctified, which means God wants us to become holy. The word holy can sound intimidating, even off-putting. For some, it brings to mind images of joyless, rule-obsessed people dressed in somber clothes, living lives defined by what they don't do. That stereotype misses the heart of what Scripture means by holiness. In the Bible, holiness isn't about being joyless or stiff.

In Scripture, the word holy carries two main ideas. To be holy means:

1. to be set apart, devoted to God and marked for his purposes.
2. being like God in character: morally pure and without sin.

Becoming holy is about belonging to God in a way that transforms the choices we make today. Holiness is not a badge you wear; it's a belonging that shapes how you live your life.

Paul isn't just giving the Thessalonians a list of do's and don'ts. He's calling them to live differently because they are different. God set them apart. They belong to God, and that changes the hierarchy of their desires.

> Sanctification is a theological word for the process of becoming holy.

It's the daily journey of learning to live like people who belong to God. Having a holy character like God is the goal, and sanctification is the path that takes us there.

As a new believer, holiness confused me. I assumed Christians were supposed to aim for perfection, and that growing in faith meant sinning less. When I first came to faith, I pictured my sin-meter as filled to the top. But if I did Christianity right, the level of that sin-meter would gradually drop until it finally hit zero in heaven. My working definition of sanctification was that becoming holy meant watching the sin-meter go down.

But how do you measure a sin-meter? What counts as progress? What if I become more humble in one area but discover pride in another? What if I grow in patience but start struggling with envy? Am I better or worse?

And does the number on the meter even matter? Let's say I've dropped from a million units of sin to half a million units— I'm still sinful. The more I tried to measure my growth, the less sense it made.

Scripture and time corrected my thinking. Holiness is about being set apart for God and learning to live as someone who belongs to him. Let's explore what it means to be set apart.

GRANDMA'S WEDDING CHINA

My grandmother kept two sets of dishes in her house. One was the everyday set, the plates we roughhousing grandkids used for everything. We didn't just eat off of them; we hauled them up the ladder to the tree house, balanced them on our knees for backyard picnics, and let the dog lick them clean when we were done. No one thought twice about it. These dishes were sturdy, practical, and always in use. They were the ordinary stuff of life.

But then there was the other set: Grandma's wedding china. The wedding china only appeared on holidays or special occasions. As a child, I was not even allowed to touch it. While the grown-ups sat at the big table set with these sparkling plates and actual silver, the kids sat at the card table with paper plates and plastic forks.

After dinner, the wedding china was never tossed in the dishwasher. It was lovingly hand washed and returned to its place of honor behind the glass cabinet doors, where its beauty could shine.

The difference was obvious even to a child. One set was ordinary, used for anything and everything. The other was set apart. It was special, used for a different purpose and treated with care and honor.

In the Bible, to sanctify something is to set it apart for a sacred use. The holy is devoted to God's use. The common is not. Holiness is not about perfection; it's about being devoted to God's purposes, set apart for his use, and seeking to live according to his values. To be holy is to be set apart, not because you're better or more fragile, but because you've been given a sacred purpose.

LIVING OUT GOD'S DESIGN

As believers, we are like that special china. We belong to God and live for a different purpose. That's why obedience matters and why our lives should look different from those who reject God. Someone watching us before and after we come to faith should see a change, not because we've become flawless, but because we belong to God and we strive to do what he says.

Eventually, we all face the big questions of life: *Who am I? What do I want to pursue in life? What is valuable to me? Who or what am I counting on?* Those aren't just philosophical questions; they reflect the priority of our desires.

As believers, we are learning to want what God wants. We no longer take our cues from culture, instinct, or convenience. Instead, we give more weight to the promises of God and what he says is true. Then we act accordingly. That's what it means to live as someone who has been set apart.

Sanctification is the pursuit of living in the light of God's truth. It begins with remembering who God is and what he has done for us through Jesus Christ. And it continues with striving to align our lives the way God says is best.

We will still fail and fall into sin. But we no longer chase a lifestyle of sin because our direction has changed. We no longer head wherever our desires lead. Instead, we run toward holiness. Growing in sanctification is about direction, not perfection.

DESIRE, AND A DIFFERENT WAY

Paul contrasts two ways of living: we either control our bodies in holiness and honor, or we give in to "the passion of lust, like those who do not know God" (1 Thessalonians 4:5).

It's easy to assume that if something feels good, it must be good. But not every desire is meant to be fulfilled. We desire many things, such as comfort, connection, security, and pleasure. Part of growing in our faith is learning the difference between what we want and what is wise, between what feels good in the moment and what God says is best.

Desire in and of itself is not wrong. Having desires is

normal. God created us with longings and desires. But he also gave us the ability to prioritize and overrule those longings.

When we want something badly enough, it can feel like a need. We tell ourselves, "I must have this. I deserve this." But that's where the test comes. Will we let our desires rule us? Or will we let our commitment to God lead us?

What separates us from animals is not the fact that we have desires. It's the fact that we can choose how we respond to our desires. Animals act on instinct.

But as human beings made in God's image, we can pause, reflect, and ask, *What's the right thing to do? I have this desire, but should I step over one of God's boundaries to fulfill it?*

The desire for food is normal. But stealing someone else's lunch is wrong. The desire to protect yourself is normal. But lying to shift blame onto someone else crosses a line. It's normal to want to succeed in your career. But betraying a friend's trust to gain that promotion comes at too high a cost.

Life gives us constant opportunities to make these kinds of choices. Becoming sanctified means learning to put our desires in proper perspective: below loving God and loving our neighbors.

Those who don't know God often follow whatever feels good in the moment. But believers live by a different motto: What would God say is right in this situation? That's our guiding desire, the one that gives shape to all the others. When we put God at the center, the rest of our longings find their proper place. Desires don't disappear, but they no longer control us.

BOUNDARIES GOD GIVES US

God's plan for us always includes boundaries. Some are universal, like the Ten Commandments. They apply to every believer in every generation. You don't need to pray about whether it's right to commit murder or adultery. That's never within bounds.

But other boundaries are personal. A married person has different boundaries than a single friend. Parents carry responsibilities that the childless lack. And a child in her parents' house faces different limitations than an adult living alone. Whatever the particulars, faithfulness means staying within the boundaries God has set for you. Outside of them, no matter how justified it feels, we're no longer trusting God.

We all face moments when the boundary feels like a barrier. We look at what others have and wonder why we can't have the same. Maybe it's a relationship, a job, or a version of life that seems easier or more exciting.

But crossing the line to grab what looks good isn't just a shift in circumstance; it's a shift in trust. It's saying, *God's not giving me what I want, so I'll take it myself.* Faith waits. Faith says, *It looks good, but my eyes deceive me. God says wait, and I will wait.*

WHAT IF I MESSED UP?

All of us have failed. The question isn't: Do you sin? You do. We all do. The question is: What do you do about it? Do you feel sorry and ask God to forgive you? Or do you shrug it off, saying, "I don't care what God thinks?"

Your temptations won't disappear overnight. Some struggles might last for years. God has his own timetable for teaching and sanctifying us. Your desires may not change tomorrow, but that's not an excuse to abandon the struggle.

At a deep level, you must want to change. You need to reach a point where you pray, "Lord, teach me to want what you say is best." God never promised that we're going to have an easy road. He promised to use our trials for a glorious purpose.

What do you do when the temptation is strong, and change feels impossible? Maybe you've thrown up your hands and said,

"I've tried. I can't change." I know many sincere believers in exactly that place.

But remember, none of us can change by sheer willpower. That's why we need a Savior. Whether your battle is with lust, greed, pride, selfishness, arrogance, or anything else, you can't erase your sin or transform your heart on your own. We need the blood of Christ to forgive us, the grace of God to hold us, and the work of the Holy Spirit to make us new.

Trust God's plan, timing, and purposes. If he asks you to carry a struggle for ten months, ten years, or a lifetime, then that's what it means for you to follow him. We don't get to choose our battles. But we can choose who we trust in the middle of them.

In modern culture, following Jesus won't get easier in the near future. But we don't follow him because it's easy. We follow him because he's worthy and because his way leads to life.

CHOOSING GOD'S WAY

Sometimes when we say, *I can't change,* what we really mean is, *I don't want to change.* That's a problem. While genuine believers struggle, at some level we want to change. We have come to a place where we say, "God's way is right, and I want to follow it, even if I keep messing up." The desire to follow God, even through failure, is a mark of saving faith.

This does not mean that if you ever succumbed to a temptation, you are not a believer. The issue isn't perfect obedience. It's your response to the truth. When God shows you where you've gone off course, are you willing to turn around?

You have a choice. Will you pursue your desires, or will you pursue God? That choice matters deeply because it reveals whether the Holy Spirit is at work in you. If you persist in a lifestyle of immorality and don't care what God thinks, that's a red flag. You're stumbling and your choices are pulling you away from God. Let that be a wake-up call.

But if you've failed, repented, and are now seeking to follow God, take heart. The blood of Jesus covers your sin. The Spirit of God is at work in you, even if the struggle remains. God isn't out to steal your joy. He wants to give you something better.

His call is to know the truth and live it, but he is also merciful. We live in the light of both of those truths. Next we'll apply them to three big problem areas: sex, work, and money.

Summary

- Our toughest temptations ultimately expose the priority of our desires and force us to choose between what we want and what God wants.
- Holiness means being set apart for God's purposes and growing in a character that reflects his moral purity, not achieving sinless perfection or ticking off rules.
- Sanctification is a daily journey of learning to live as people who belong to God.
- Because holiness is about belonging, our desires must take second place to God's commands and promises.
- Desire itself is not sinful, but acting on desire outside God-given boundaries is wrong.
- God provides universal boundaries (e.g., the Ten Commandments) and personal boundaries (shaped by our season of life) to guide faithful living within his design.
- When we cross those boundaries, the issue is not whether we sin (we all do) but how we respond: genuine believers repent, seek God's help, and keep wrestling toward obedience.

- Lasting change is impossible by sheer willpower; we depend on Christ's atoning work, God's grace, and the Holy Spirit's transforming power to forgive, sustain, and reshape us.
- Persistent indifference to God's standards is a warning sign of divided loyalty, while ongoing struggle paired with repentance is evidence of the Spirit's work.

See for Yourself

Galatians 5:13–24; 1 Corinthians 6:9–20; Romans 11:33–12:3; 1 Peter 2:1–10

Reflection

When a strong desire tugs at you, what principle or authority do you consult before acting? Is that desire truly leading you toward the life you want?

10

SEX

TRUSTING GOD WITH DESIRE

For this is the will of God, your sanctification: that you abstain from sexual immorality; that each one of you know how to control his own body in holiness and honor, not in the passion of lust like the Gentiles who do not know God; that no one transgress and wrong his brother in this matter, because the Lord is an avenger in all these things, as we told you beforehand and solemnly warned you.

— 1 THESSALONIANS 4:3–6

What do King David, the ancient Thessalonians and Corinthians, church leaders throughout history, and many of us today have in common? At some point, we've all wrestled with what God says about sex.

That struggle isn't new, and it's not random. Sexuality is one of the most powerful and deeply personal aspects of being human. It's also one of the easiest places to wander off track.

One area where Christians are called to live very differently from the surrounding culture is in how we handle our sexuality.

Following God means turning away from any sexual behavior that goes against or falls outside of God's design.

THE BLUEPRINT

What is God's plan for sex? Looking at the Bible as a whole, we see a clear, consistent picture: sexuality is a good and beautiful part of how God created us. From the beginning, God designed sex to be enjoyed within the covenant of marriage, a lifelong, monogamous relationship between one man and one woman.

Within that covenant, sex is a gift. It deepens intimacy, strengthens trust, expresses love, and brings new life into the world. Outside that covenant, sex no longer reflects God's design. Simply put:

> God's design for sex is chastity before marriage and fidelity after.

Our culture often treats sex as a private choice or purely physical act with no meaning. Scripture paints a different view. Sex is never merely physical. By its very nature, sex involves relationship, trust, and vulnerability. It creates emotional and spiritual ties. That's part of God's design.

God gave it meaning on purpose. It's not only about pleasure or procreation. It's the language of marriage, meant to say with our bodies what our vows say with our words: "I will share my life with you and only you."

When Paul tells the Thessalonians to abstain from sexual immorality, he's telling them to avoid every form of sexual activity outside the covenant of marriage, including premarital sex, adultery, pornography, and same-sex sexual relationships.

Scripture is clear. Scripture consistently affirms sex is a good gift, to be enjoyed in marriage the way God intended:

Chastity before marriage to one person of the opposite sex. Fidelity after.

In Paul's day, people married younger than today. Their biggest challenge wasn't deciding whether to marry; their challenge was remaining faithful after marriage. Paul urges them to control their bodies in holiness and honor as opposed to pursuing every desire like those who don't know God (1 Thessalonians 4:2–6).

Controlling our bodies "in holiness and honor" is striving to live in the ways that God says is right. A life of sexual integrity is one that you can live in the open. If all your actions became public, there would be no shame, no regret, and no trail of hurt. You wouldn't need to lie or sneak around. Nor would you use someone else for your own pleasure. Instead, you conduct yourself with honesty and dignity, openly before both God and others.

INTEGRITY HAS NO LOOPHOLES

Being single doesn't mean that the rules don't apply. There's no loophole that says singles can do whatever they want until they get engaged. Married, single, divorced, or widowed, your sexual choices still matter. Our choices shape future marriages, alter how we trust, and change the way we relate to one another.

Just because something is consensual doesn't mean that it's harmless. If you sleep with someone else's spouse or someone who may one day be someone else's spouse, you've caused harm, even if no one else knows it yet (1 Thessalonians 4:6).

The idea that our private choices can't harm anyone else is a lie. What we do with our bodies affects more than just ourselves. Just because a practice is culturally accepted doesn't mean it honors God.

Holiness calls us to ask deeper questions like:

- Does this choice reflect who I am in Christ?
- Does it honor the other person and/or the person I might one day marry?
- Does it align with God's purposes and design?

Sexual integrity isn't about shame or restriction. It's about learning to love others rightly and to live in a way that brings honor rather than regret.

Do I Trust God Here?

Sexuality is such a powerful and pleasurable part of life that it quickly becomes a test of faith. It's easy to think: *My situation is so different, surely, God's rules don't apply to me.* Maybe your desire feels overwhelming. Or your spouse let you down. Or your loneliness feels sharper than anyone else could understand.

But Paul doesn't make exceptions. He's writing to a church of genuine believers, and he speaks plainly: God's design applies to all of us.

Sex was created to bond a married couple together and build a family. When we step outside of that design, we aren't just breaking a rule. We're rejecting God's wisdom, harming ourselves and others in the process.

In those moments when our desires pull us toward something outside his boundaries, we face a question of trust: *Do I really believe God's way is best, even when it's hard?*

Not Man, But God

Paul anticipates pushback. He knows some will write him off as old-fashioned or irrelevant. But he doesn't leave room for personal opinion here. "Whoever disregards this," he says, "disregards not man but God" (1 Thessalonians 4:8).

If we reject what Paul says about sexuality, we're not just

disagreeing with an apostle. We're rejecting the One who created us.

God himself set the boundaries around sexuality. He designed it to thrive within the commitment of marriage between one man and one woman. Our choice is whether we will submit to that design.

To deny that God has a design for sexuality is to rebel against him. We can't say we trust Jesus to save us, then turn around and ignore what he says about how we should live.

We need Jesus because we've all gone wrong, sexually and otherwise. Repentance is a full turn. We can't turn halfway and still cling to a few sins we want to keep for ourselves. "Jesus, save me from my sin" means we give him our entire selves, not just the parts we're comfortable letting go.

Sin distorts our thinking and pulls us off course. We need God to renew our minds, not just our actions. Following Jesus means learning to trust him in every area, including our sexuality.

SUMMARY

- Scripture consistently portrays sex as a good and beautiful gift, meant to flourish only within the lifelong, monogamous covenant of marriage between one man and one woman.
- The divine pattern is chastity before marriage and fidelity after marriage.
- Paul's command to abstain from sexual immorality forbids premarital sex, adultery, pornography, and same-sex sexual relations—any act that lies outside biblical marriage.
- Genuine sexual integrity can be lived openly, without secrecy, shame, or exploitation of another person.

See for Yourself

1 Thessalonians 4:1–12; Genesis 2; Matthew 5:27–30; Proverbs 5:15–20

Reflection

Where do you feel the biggest tension between God's design for sexuality and today's cultural norms? How do you navigate that?

11

WORK

SERVING GOD IN DAILY LIFE

... But we urge you, brothers, to do this more and more, and to aspire to live quietly, and to mind your own affairs, and to work with your hands, as we instructed you, so that you may walk properly before outsiders and be dependent on no one.

—1 THESSALONIANS 4:10–12

Work might not seem like a spiritual issue, but it is another enormous area where following Jesus sets us apart. How we work reflects how we value others, and where we place our trust. When Paul wrote to the Thessalonians, he made this connection clear (1 Thessalonians 4:9–12; 2 Thessalonians 3:6–15).

Like sexuality, how we work reveals what we want most. If we shrug off our chores and let someone else carry our load, we are putting ourselves first. But when we do the task in front of us, whether it's changing a diaper, balancing a budget, or sweeping a shop floor, our efforts become a daily way to love our neighbors.

Work is more than earning a paycheck or building a career. From the beginning, God asked us to work and keep his world (Genesis 2:15). That call still stands. A salary not only feeds your household; faithful work can also bless your coworkers, customers, and community. Work is about taking responsibility and doing what needs to be done for the sake of those around us.

DAILY GRIND, DAILY LOVE

Back in Thessalonica, some believers had stopped working altogether. They believed Jesus would return at any moment, so they saw no need to continue their everyday responsibilities. Instead of contributing, they depended on others in the church for support.

Eventually, the situation grew so disruptive that the church wrote to Paul asking what to do. Paul urged every able-bodied person to live quietly, mind their own business, and earn their own living so they depended on no one (1 Thessalonians 4:10–12).

When the problem continued, he wrote a second letter and spoke more directly: "If anyone is not willing to work, let him not eat" (2 Thessalonians 3:10).

That may sound harsh, but Paul was not condemning those who *could* not work. He was addressing those who *would* not work. The deeper issue concerns the place of desire, responsibility, and loving others. When we contribute nothing and instead expect others to take care of us, we are using our neighbors, not loving them.

THE LIE OF THE EASY LIFE

Like sexuality, the heart of this issue is how we respond to desire. Most people long for an easy life, a shortcut to security, and a way to skip the hard stuff and still come out ahead. If that's our primary goal, letting others carry our load might seem like a clever solution.

But it's not a loving solution. It's not even wise. God didn't design us to drift through life while someone else does all of our work. He calls us to contribute. Since we are all equal before him, he expects us to step into the roles and responsibilities he's given us with faith and humility.

When you work, you're doing more than earning a living. You are taking care of the people you love by supporting them and not becoming a burden on them. You are showing respect for their needs, acknowledging that your needs are no more important than theirs, and doing your part so they're not left to carry you.

Refusing to work when you can isn't freedom; it's selfishness. It's putting your needs above others. But when you choose to work faithfully, even in small or unseen ways, you are living out what it means to love your neighbor as yourself.

Work doesn't have to earn a paycheck to be work. Parenting, homemaking, and caring for elderly parents may not come with salaries, but they are real and valuable work. They reflect the same principle: using your time and energy to contribute to the needs of your family and meet your responsibilities. Whether you're managing a household or a team, you are working to meet the responsibilities God has given you.

A Day in the Life of a Servant of God

Let me tell you a story from the Old Testament (2 Samuel 17). While David was king of Israel, his son Absalom rebelled. Warned of Absalom's growing support, David fled Jerusalem with his household and loyal servants. Behind him, he left three key allies: his advisor Hushai and the priests Zadok and Abiathar.

Absalom quickly seized the throne, but one obstacle remained: his father was still alive. When Absalom's advisors devised a plan to hunt David down, Absalom shared the scheme with Hushai, unaware he was confiding in a double agent.

Hushai passed the news to the two priests, who entrusted it to an unnamed maidservant. Cleverly disguised as a woman doing her daily chores, she slipped through the city gates undetected and headed for a spring outside Jerusalem, where the priests' sons, Jonathan and Ahimaaz, waited.

Here their plan seemed to be foiled. A sharp-eyed onlooker spotted their exchange and sent word back to Absalom. The chase was on. Jonathan and Ahimaaz raced across the countryside finding refuge at a farmhouse.

There, another unnamed woman lowered them into an empty well, covered the opening with a rug, and scattered grain on top. When Absalom's men pounded on her door, she sent them in the wrong direction.

After the danger passed, the two messengers climbed out, crossed the Jordan under cover of night, and delivered the warning to King David. David moved his people to safety just as sunrise painted the eastern sky.

All these people risked certain death to aid David. Taken together they look like a motley crew of nobodies. None of them wore armor or held impressive titles. They were both male and female, some educated and some probably not. They held both secular and priestly jobs.

What did they have in common? They faithfully did what God asked them to do.

In the midst of a royal crisis, God preserved his chosen king and his larger promises through the quiet obedience of a government worker, two priests, their sons, a maidservant, and a quick-thinking farm wife at a well.

But none of them knew they were making biblical history.

They just did what they were called to do on the day they were called to do it.

Living Quietly: Trusting God's Plan

With that backdrop, Paul's exhortation to the Thessalonians to "aspire to live quietly" (1 Thessalonians 4:11) comes into sharper focus, showing us that kingdom work is rarely about headlines but is always about steady, deliberate obedience.

At first glance, aspiring to live quietly sounds like a contradiction. Quiet lives don't get headlines. Ambition is usually about climbing corporate ladders, chasing goals, and standing out. But Paul's point isn't about shrinking back or settling. It's about learning to live faithfully within the calling God gives you, no more, no less.

There's no list of "kingdom jobs" that matter more to God than others. Honest work, whatever form it takes, is valuable. Providing for your family and stewarding your responsibilities well is kingdom work. Most of the time, doing what's right in front of you is exactly what faithfulness to God looks like.

> Living quietly means accepting the boundaries God sets and finding peace within them.

It's not resignation, it's trust. It's saying, "This is the road God gave me, and I believe he knows best." We avoid the paths he's warned us about. We wait when he says wait. We move forward when he opens the way.

We describe this as our vocation or calling. God has a role for each of us, but he rarely hands us a five-year plan. More often, he shows us only the next step. We trust that he will guide us where we need to go, even if we can't yet see all the turns in the road ahead.

IMPACT VS OBEDIENCE

It's ironic that the apostle Paul is the one who tells us to live quietly. Few people have had a greater impact on the world than he did. Yet his life reflected the very principle he taught. When Paul entered a new city, he preached in the synagogue and he sewed tents to support himself. He shared the gospel when the door opened, and he trusted God with the results.

That trust didn't shield him from hardship. He was often beaten, arrested, or driven out of town. But while recovering or sitting in jail, he wrote letters that now form much of the New Testament. Through those letters, Paul has shaped the lives of millions. But he didn't aim for that kind of legacy. He simply did the next faithful thing.

Living quietly doesn't mean that we won't make an impact. It means our goal isn't to be the one who changes the world; it's to be faithful to the One who is changing it. We act on what we've been taught, and we let God decide what results will come from it.

There's nothing wrong with dreaming of a job that excites you. That's natural. But it's worth asking: *Do I want to see good things happen? Or do I want to be the one who makes them happen?*

Paul's call to a quiet life is an invitation to let God be God. It's his kingdom. We each have a part to play, but the story doesn't depend on us. Our role is to love the people God placed in front of us and stay faithful in the calling he's given us, whatever that looks like. Instead of striving for impact, aim for faithful obedience.

OBEDIENCE OVER AMBITION

Today, some folks claim you should never settle for a job that isn't fulfilling. The assumption is that if a job is not prestigious or creatively stimulating, then it's not worth doing. If God gives you a job that energizes you and matches your passions, be thankful. That's a wonderful gift.

But if the only door open is a job that simply puts food on the table, take it. Do it well for God. You can serve God in a "regular" job, too.

Paul modeled this himself. Though he traveled and preached the gospel, he didn't rely on charity. He made tents to support himself. When he stayed with the Thessalonians, he worked to avoid giving the impression that he was making money off the gospel.

Would it have been easier for Paul to preach full-time and leave tent making behind? Absolutely. But Paul chose the harder road to teach by example. He showed that loving others sometimes means working quietly and carrying your own weight.

The motivation here is not "get a job and get your act together." It is "believe the gospel and live like it's true." In the end, the motivation is trusting God's wisdom even when the world contradicts him.

Yes, sexual immorality and financial irresponsibility can cause harm and have serious consequences. But underneath both is a deeper issue: rejecting the authority of the God who defines what is right and wrong. And that rejection is far more dangerous than any short-term mistake. That's a matter of the soul.

Of course, God shows grace, mercy, and forgiveness for anyone who repents and runs to him. He offers abundant and overflowing grace. The underlying issue behind work is: Do you want what God wants? Do you trust his promises more than you trust your own desires? Are you content to live within the boundaries he has lovingly set?

Work isn't only about survival or making a name for yourself. It's about trust and love. Living quietly isn't settling; it's obedience. Do what's in front of you. Be faithful where you are. And let God take care of the rest.

While work is a tangible way to love our neighbors, money tests who we trust once the paycheck arrives. Next we'll tackle how followers of Jesus handle the wealth he puts in our hands.

SUMMARY

- Work is an act of love and trust, not merely a means of survival or self-promotion.
- God ordained work as a means of stewarding his creation; work is one aspect of that broader calling.
- Conscientious labor, whether diaper-changing, number-crunching, or floor-sweeping, is a daily act of neighbor-love that lifts the burden from others rather than shifting it onto them.
- Living quietly means embracing the boundaries God assigns and trusting him with both opportunities and outcomes.
- God values honest work of every kind; there is no special list of "kingdom jobs" that count more than others.
- The deeper question behind our work is whether we will accept God's authority over our desires and trust his wisdom above our own.

SEE FOR YOURSELF

1 Thessalonians 4:9–12; 2 Thessalonians 3:1–18; Proverbs 6:6–11, 21:25, 24:30–34; Colossians 3:18–4:1

REFLECTION

How does viewing work as part of loving your neighbor challenge or affirm your current view of your job and daily responsibilities?

12

MONEY

TRUSTING GOD, NOT WEALTH

Take care, and be on your guard against all covetousness, for one's life does not consist in the abundance of his possessions.

— LUKE 12:15

We've talked about sex and work. Let's tackle the third topic most people avoid at the dinner table: money.

Like sex and work, money plays a powerful role in our lives. It's necessary, it's complicated, and it often reveals more about our values than we'd like to admit. If you want to follow Jesus in a real, day-to-day way, you can't ignore how you handle your finances. Thankfully, Scripture doesn't ignore it either.

As with sexuality and work, the problem with money is not having it; it's loving it too much (1 Timothy 6:9–10; Hebrews 13:5). Jesus makes this clear in the Sermon on the Mount.

No one can serve two masters, for either he will hate the one and love the other, or he will be devoted to the one and despise the other. You cannot serve God and money (Matthew 6:24).

When God speaks, we rightly obey. God as master makes sense. But how is wealth our master? Since wealth is not a person, it cannot give us commands or instructions.

THE INVISIBLE MASTER YOU OBEY

Imagine life as a household servant in Jesus' day. The master punished servants who resisted his will but rewarded those who complied. The master's approval or displeasure shaped the servant's daily life.

In today's world, wealth functions much the same way. It hands out rewards and penalties. If you manage money wisely (saving for unknowns and spending within your means) wealth treats you well, granting a measure of security and peace. Ignore its basic rules, and the consequences can feel like punishment: debt, anxiety, and lost opportunities.

When you become a slave to wealth, the consequences can be grim. Chasing money devours time and energy. It demands sacrifices to climb the corporate ladder, such as flattering the right bosses, backstabbing rivals, and skipping family dinners to get ahead. In that sense, wealth behaves like a master who enforces his own household code.

Likewise, God has a set of expectations. We could call them his household rules. He instructs us to love our neighbor as ourselves, to trust that he will keep his promises, and to live within the boundaries he has given us, weaving generosity, kindness, and mercy into the fabric of our daily lives.

The pursuit of wealth demands one set of loyalties; the pursuit of God requires another. You can't pledge allegiance to both. To receive the blessing of our master, we must serve him well.

Playing for Both Teams

Still, you may wonder, *Why can't we serve both God and wealth?* After all, many people successfully juggle two jobs without conflict. For example, many people work part time for the city and part time in the private sector as consultants. Serving two human bosses isn't inherently problematic because both ultimately want the same thing: your productive labor in exchange for a paycheck.

But sometimes a genuine conflict of interest emerges. Imagine that in your government post you write the regulations that govern wineries, and in your second job, you own and operate a winery.

Now the two masters pull you in opposite directions. A decision that helps your private business could undercut your public duties. Likewise, a ruling that protects the public interest might cost your own winery money. Eventually, you'll have to choose which master to please, helping one while harming the other.

That tension is what Jesus means when he speaks of "hating" one master and "loving" the other. As we've seen, in biblical language, love is working for someone's good, while hate is working against them. Sooner or later you have to pick a side and "love" one master by serving his interests and "hate" the other by blocking his. Inevitably, a conflict of interest will arise between loving wealth and loving God. Your response exposes where your true loyalties lie.

Loyal, Not Poor

Scripture never condemns honest work or material wealth. As we saw, Paul insists that able-bodied people work for a living. Providing for yourself and your family is praiseworthy, and prosperity is not inherently sinful. Many devoted believers (e.g., Abraham, Job, or Lydia) were well-off. Poverty and abundance each bring their own temptations; neither condition is holier by default.

The issue, once again, is the place of desire. Believers are learning to treasure God's will and his promises more than the riches this world offers. The question is not how much you can earn but who you trust no matter what that amount is.

Sooner or later, that loyalty will be tested. Clinging to the promises of God may require loosening your grip on possessions. When the moment comes, your choice will reveal whether you serve the Giver or the gifts.

This divided loyalty ensnared the Pharisees in Jesus' day and explains why he rebuked them so sharply. They spoke about honoring God and keeping the Law, yet their hearts craved what the world could give: money, status, and the applause of their peers.

Instead of letting God's commands shape them, they searched for loopholes, doing whatever it took to advance their own prosperity while preserving a facade of keeping the Law. Given a choice between obeying God and protecting their social standing, they chose worldly gain every time.

Fundamentally, we are designed for worship, or as Jesus puts it, to serve a master. Everyone will serve something or someone: it might be sex, work, money, beauty, or a political cause. But only one master is worthy. The God who created you wants you to worship and love him, and he wants to love you back. He is a wise and compassionate master.

If all this seems overwhelming, the good news is you're not

in it alone. You have an ally. We'll meet him in the following chapter.

SUMMARY

- How we handle money exposes our deepest loyalties and desires.
- Although money is not a person, it "masters" us by dispensing rewards (security, comfort) and punishments (debt, anxiety) that shape daily choices.
- A conflict of interest will arise between loving wealth and loving God, forcing us to choose who we serve.
- Scripture never condemns honest labor or material prosperity; it condemns the love of money.
- The decisive issue is whom we trust: God the Giver or the gifts he provides.

SEE FOR YOURSELF

Deuteronomy 8:11–18; Matthew 6:19–24; Luke 12:15–21; Proverbs 3:9–10; 11:24–28; 30:7–9

REFLECTION

When a financial opportunity conflicts with your core principles, which side wins? What does that choice reveal about what you ultimately trust?

PART IV

FINISHING STRONG

1 3

THE HOLY SPIRIT

YOUR HELPER IN THE CHRISTIAN LIFE

In him you also, when you heard the word of truth, the gospel of your salvation, and believed in him, were sealed with the promised Holy Spirit, who is the guarantee of our inheritance until we acquire possession of it, to the praise of his glory.

— EPHESIANS 1:13–14

When you're new to Christianity, it's easy to feel overwhelmed. There's so much to learn, and life doesn't suddenly become easy just because you believe in Jesus. In fact, you may ask, *How will I keep going?*

The good news is you aren't fighting the battle alone. After sending his Son to deal with your guilt, God sent his Spirit to ensure your victory. The Holy Spirit is more than a helper or guide. He's a promise etched into your soul, a mark that says, "This one belongs to God." He's the guarantee that your salvation is real and that you'll make it to the finish line.

A Promise Made Long Ago

By giving us his Spirit, God fulfilled a promise that reaches all the way back to the Old Testament.

- Moses longed for the day when everyone, not just prophets or leaders, would receive the Spirit (Numbers 11:28–29).
- Jeremiah spoke of a time when God would write his Law directly on the hearts of his people (Jeremiah 31:33–34).
- Ezekiel predicted God would take away our hearts of stone and give us hearts of flesh (Ezekiel 36:26–27).
- And Joel envisioned a day when men and women, young and old, from every background, would all receive the Spirit of God (Joel 2:28–29).

What Moses longed for and the prophets proclaimed came to pass on the day of Pentecost. After his resurrection, Jesus told his apostles to wait in Jerusalem. He said they would soon be baptized with the Holy Spirit (Acts 1:1–8). As they gathered for the Jewish feast of Pentecost, a sound like rushing wind filled the room and flames appeared above their heads.

Suddenly, they began speaking about the mighty works of God in languages they had never learned, but which were understood by the crowds who had come to Jerusalem from all over the world.

Then Peter, the same man who had denied Jesus mere weeks before, stood up and spoke with boldness. He explained the meaning of Jesus' death and resurrection, and three thousand people believed the gospel and were baptized (Acts 2:1–41).

At Pentecost, God fulfilled the promises of the Old Testament in a dramatic and personal way. Now God's Spirit changes all of his people from the inside out. Instead of trying to obey

God's commands by sheer willpower and law-keeping, the Holy Spirit fixes our broken choosers, so we start to choose what God wants. Slowly but surely, our lives begin to reflect God's character because his Spirit is transforming us, not because we're striving harder.

THE SEAL THAT CLAIMS YOU

Paul describes believers as being sealed by the Spirit (Ephesians 1:13). To understand what that means, picture a scene from medieval times. A king sits at his desk, signing an important letter. He drips hot wax onto the parchment and presses his ring, engraved with a unique royal crest, into the wax.

That seal does more than close the letter. It identifies the document as authentic, shows it belongs to the king, and guarantees it is under the king's protection. Only the intended recipient may break the seal. If anyone else tampers with it, he might lose his head.

That's the image Paul draws on to describe believers. When you believe the gospel, God stamps you with his Spirit.

The seal of the Holy Spirit carries the same three meanings: authenticity, ownership, and protection.

Having the Spirit proves you have genuine saving faith. You don't need a certificate or a church document to prove you're a Christian. If God has pressed his signet ring against your soul as evidenced by his Spirit at work within you, you are the real deal.

The seal also means that you belong to God. In his letters, Paul often divides humanity into two groups: those who belong to God, and those who don't. As we saw in Chapter 7, one way we know we belong is that we proclaim, "Jesus is Lord." That confession is evidence of the Spirit at work in us, reshaping our loyalties and opening our eyes to the truth. Having the Spirit testifies that we are God's.

Just as important, the seal is a promise of protection. In ancient times, it was against the law to break the king's seal or contradict his edicts. The seal carried the full weight of the king's authority. Paul uses that imagery to assure us that when God seals us with his Spirit, no one can snatch us away from him, not even us. God declares, "This one is mine," and that declaration stands for eternity.

Paul also describes the Holy Spirit as a pledge of our future inheritance (Ephesians 1:14). A pledge is like earnest money in a real estate transaction. If I promise to buy your house, I give you a deposit up front. That deposit guarantees I'm serious. It's a sign that I intend to follow through and pay the full amount. The Holy Spirit is that kind of pledge. When God gives us his Spirit, he's saying, "I fully intend to bring you into the fullness of your salvation."

Because of Jesus, God adopts us into his family. As his children, God promises we will inherit a place in his eternal kingdom. We don't possess that inheritance yet; it's still to come. But the Spirit guarantees God will do what he has promised. He's not just offering us hope; he's securing it. Right now, we wait. But we wait with confidence, because the Spirit at work in us is proof that God's promises are already underway.

Our inheritance is a future inheritance because God has not fully redeemed us yet. We still struggle with sin and live in a fallen world. But even so, our destiny is sealed. God has claimed us, and he will carry us across the finish line. The presence of the Holy Spirit in our lives assures us we will make it home. But how does the Spirit work?

~

A Wind You Can't Tame

Late one night, Nicodemus quietly approached Jesus (John 3:1–21). Nicodemus was a Pharisee (a Jewish religious teacher) and a ruler among the Jews. Jesus intrigued him, but he didn't want the other Pharisees to see his interest. They already suspected that Jesus was a fraud.

Nicodemus was not so sure. He came under cover of darkness, hoping to find answers. But instead of giving simple explanations, Jesus introduced an idea that left him more confused: "You must be born again."

Nicodemus was baffled. *Born again? How could anyone crawl back into the womb? That couldn't be right.*

From his religious training, the path to salvation was clear: be born Jewish, and keep the Law. In that system, your physical birth matters. Who your parents are determines your inheritance. If your father is Jewish, then you stand to inherit the promises given to Abraham, so long as you also follow the Old Testament Law.

But Jesus told him that Jewish birthright wasn't enough. The problem runs deeper. Jewish or not, everyone inherits more than a name or a tribe. We inherit a broken chooser. A better rulebook or a more sincere effort won't fix that. We need a spiritual rebirth. To enter the kingdom of God, we must be born from above.

That new birth happens when God gives you his Spirit. Just like your physical birth made you part of your earthly family, this spiritual birth brings you into God's family. It's not something you can manufacture. It's something God does for you.

While Nicodemus marveled at this answer, Jesus continued:

The wind blows where it wishes, and you hear its sound, but you don't know where it comes from or where it goes. So it is with everyone who is born of the Spirit (John 3:8).

Picture it. You're outside on a still afternoon when a breeze suddenly sweeps through. You didn't see it coming, and you can't predict where it's headed. But you hear the rustle of leaves, feel it tug at your hair, and watch the trees sway. You can't direct the wind, but you can see its effects. That's how the Spirit works: invisible, unstoppable, and moving on God's terms, not ours.

Some folks think that the Holy Spirit is a power you tap into, like 'the Force' in Star Wars. But Jesus does not describe the Spirit as a force we master. He compares the Spirit to the wind: free, sovereign, and untamed. You can't summon him with the right words. You can't bend him to your will. The Spirit moves when and how he wants as God wills. And when he does, you see the results, not because you orchestrated it, but because your life has changed.

That's hard for many of us to accept. We've been trained to believe that if we just try hard enough, we can make anything happen. We're often told that if we want to be better Christians, we simply need to master the right disciplines and learn the right methods.

But that's not how spiritual growth works. Becoming more like Christ isn't about technique. It's about transformation. And transformation is the Spirit's work, not ours.

Our role isn't to control the Spirit; it's to trust him. The Spirit doesn't wait for us to say the perfect prayer before he moves. His hands are not tied until we unlock some secret formula. He's like the wind, moving when and where he chooses, bringing about the changes God has planned. Any transformation we produce through sheer willpower is temporary and superficial. Only the Spirit can produce lasting change.

Think about what this idea meant for Nicodemus. He came to Jesus expecting clarity and left with a challenge to rethink everything. He thought that salvation came through heritage and effort.

But Jesus said it required something he couldn't produce: rebirth. At first, that must have felt disorienting. If birthright doesn't save and keeping the Law isn't enough, then who can be saved? What can anyone do to be born again?

Jesus' answer is simple and freeing: We do nothing to be born again. God gives it to us as a gift. The Holy Spirit is God's invisible agent of change. He moves as God directs, bringing new life where there was none. When the Spirit moves, lasting transformation results. Jesus calls that being born again.

That transformation starts with the most important change of all: the gift of saving faith. The Spirit opens our eyes so that we can see and understand the truth. I call this gift of faith the universal work of the Spirit, because every believer experiences it.

But the Spirit also works in other ways, what I call his individual works. These are the unique roles, gifts, and opportunities he gives to each of us in order to help us serve the body of Christ.

GIFTS FOR THE GREATER GOOD

Imagine a kitchen buzzing with motion. A chef moves with confidence, creating a culinary masterpiece. Around him, assistants chop vegetables of every color you can imagine. Others grate spices that scent the air, while someone else minces herbs into tiny green flecks. You hear meat sizzling on a grill as a cook bastes it with a rich, dark sauce. Eventually, the chef combines every unique ingredient into a savory stew that's complex, rich, and deeply satisfying.

That's a picture of how the Holy Spirit works in the community of people who believe in Jesus. Just as each ingredient plays a part in the meal, each believer has a part to play in God's kingdom. The Spirit gives different roles to different people on purpose. No one has every gift, and no one is meant to. Like a chef selecting the right mix for the perfect dish, God blends our lives and gifts together to create something better than we could ever produce alone.

The Corinthians, the same group that was confused about speaking in tongues, needed help in understanding spiritual gifts (1 Corinthians 12–14). They looked around at the diversity and variety of gifts and assumed something was wrong. They assumed that those without the gift of tongues must be missing the Spirit. To them, unity meant sameness.

But Paul tells them the opposite. Diversity isn't a sign of disorder; it's part of God's design. Not everyone is meant to speak in tongues. Some will teach while others serve. Some will lead while others will encourage. Everyone has a role, and all of them matter. The Spirit distributes these gifts as the Father dictates, not for our status, but for the good of the whole.

To help the Corinthians understand, Paul uses a familiar example: the human body (1 Corinthians 12:12–13). Our physical bodies have many parts: hands, eyes, ears, feet, all distinct, all necessary. No one part does everything, but each one contributes to the whole. Together, the parts form a single unified body. That's how the church works. Individual believers are like body parts, each one unique, but all joined together in Christ.

The Spirit unifies us (1 Corinthians 12:15–25). Just as your body is unified collection of parts, the church is one body made up of many members. You don't think of your hand or eye as separate from you. They are part of who you are. Likewise, we shouldn't think of ourselves as isolated individuals. We belong to something bigger.

Instead of judging each other based on which gifts we have or wishing we had someone else's, we can rejoice that we're part of the same body. The body depends on our differences. A body wouldn't function if it were missing half its parts, or if every part tried to do the same job. What makes the body work is that each part plays its role. That's how we should think about the church: no ranking, no jealousy, and no dismissing one role as less important than another.

The Corinthians turned spiritual gifts into a contest, bragging about what they had, or wishing for what they didn't. But that's like your eye saying, "I'm better than the hand." It doesn't make sense. The hand and the eye aren't in competition. They're made to work together. Just like a healthy body needs all its parts, the church needs all its members. And the Spirit is the one who creates that diversity on purpose, for our good and for God's glory.

SERVING, NOT SHOWING OFF

Picture a toolbox loaded with a large variety of tools: hammers, screwdrivers, wrenches, and pliers. Each one is necessary for a different job. When God gives you a spiritual gift, it's not meant to hang on the wall and be admired. It's meant to be used.

The Holy Spirit equips each of us not so we can show off, but so we can serve. Our gifts aren't for making a name for ourselves. They're for building up the body of Christ and helping bring about God's kingdom.

Peter puts it simply:

As each has received a gift, use it to serve one another, as good stewards of God's varied grace (1 Peter 4:10).

The word translated "varied" or "manifold" means multifaceted, like a diamond catching light from every angle. God's grace shines through us in a thousand different ways, and our gifts are how we reflect that grace to others. We serve not for our own benefit, but as stewards, people entrusted with something valuable on behalf of someone greater.

ROLES, NOT SUPERPOWERS

But too often, we twist this idea. We treat spiritual gifts like spiritual superpowers, something we unlock at conversion to impress others. *I have the gift of teaching, so I need to be in the spotlight.* Or we let them limit what we do. *Helping isn't my thing, so I'm off the hook.*

That kind of thinking misses the point. The Corinthians struggled with this, too. They bragged about who spoke in tongues and looked down on those who didn't. But the Spirit isn't passing out trophies. He's assigning roles. Gifts are not about making you look good; they are about helping the church function well.

After reminding the Corinthians that the Spirit works in a variety of ways, Paul gives examples of specific gifts (1 Corinthians 12:28). But we often misunderstand the purpose of his list. We treat his lists like a catalog to study so we can identify which gift we have.

But Paul isn't writing a guidebook for finding your personal superpower. He is explaining how the Spirit works, and then he lists a few examples. His point is to highlight the diversity of roles in the church and the unity of the Spirit behind them.

In fact, every time Paul lists spiritual gifts, the list is different. That's a clue that his purpose isn't classification. His goal is to show that the Spirit works in many ways. The lists serve a larger point: unity in diversity, and a call to serve one another in love.

LISTS, NOT LABELS

Many in modern church culture have developed a technical understanding of spiritual gifts, which misunderstands Paul and unnecessarily limits the way we use our gifts. This common misunderstanding goes something like this: spiritual gifts are supernatural abilities that God gives believers at conversion. These spiritual gifts are distinct from natural talents. We believers need to discover which gifts God gave us to fulfill our calling.

Sometimes spiritual gifts are distinguished from natural talents or skills. If a person has leadership, hospitality, or communication skills before coming to faith, some think those skills cannot be part of his or her spiritual gifts. They define spiritual gifts as special, divine powers given at the moment of conversion and do not believe they can be developed through practice or hard work.

This view often assumes there's a fixed list of gifts (usually drawn from 1 Corinthians 12:8–10, Romans 12:6–8, and Ephesians 4:11–13) and that each believer has one primary gift and a few supporting ones. The gifts are usually seen as easily categorized and clearly defined.

In practice, this model often limits how believers serve. People think, *I can't do that; it's not my gift.* Or, *I have the gift of leadership, so I should be in charge.* It creates categories and hierarchies that Paul never intended. In this popular framework, spiritual gifts become fixed traits, like personality types, that define what we can or can't do in the church.

But Paul isn't trying to limit what believers can do. He's pointing to the many ways that God enables us to serve and how those roles can change depending on the needs of the body and the leading of the Spirit. In the passages where Paul talks about gifts, he's not laying out a spiritual personality test. He's talking about how God equips us to serve one another in practical ways.

What Paul describes isn't a list of divine talents. It's a description of roles, responsibilities, and opportunities to serve. These aren't gifts in the sense of unique superpowers. They're gifts in the sense of assignments and ways God invites us to participate in his work. The Spirit isn't handing out abilities to showcase, but individual callings to step into.

STEP INTO THE OPPORTUNITY

So how do you find your roles? It's not about training with a Jedi Master or taking a quiz. Instead, look around and ask a simple question: How can I serve others? God is already bringing you opportunities. You don't need special discernment; simply look for a job that needs doing and try doing it.

These opportunities are among the many gifts God gives us. He doesn't need your help to accomplish his will, but he invites you to participate anyway. Each of us has a unique place to reflect Christ's love, to proclaim the gospel, and to serve others. And because every life situation is different, the number of roles is effectively limitless. God isn't bound by a list. He's shaping you for the opportunities he places in front of you.

If God gives you opportunities to teach, then obediently practice, study, and improve your teaching. The opportunity to teach is the gift, not a supernatural ability to teach. God often gives us opportunities related to our natural talents, interests and abilities, because those natural abilities are part of God's gifts, too. He often gives us the desires and skills to fulfill the task he's called us to. But he could also challenge you to do something new.

You don't need to take tests or stress about finding your "official" gifts. Try something and see what happens. In fact, try several things and see what happens. Help in ways that feel natural and in ways that stretch you.

> Rather than asking, *What's my gift?* try asking, *What opportunities has God given me today?*

Your opportunities will probably change over time. You might serve in one way during your twenties and in an entirely different way in your fifties. That's not a failure; that's growth. Using our gifts is not about being the most impressive tool in the toolbox. It's about being faithful. We're not solo acts. We're a team. So grab your tool, serve someone, and watch what God builds through you.

But what about those days when it's overwhelming and you're tempted to give up? We'll talk about that next.

Summary

- Paul likens the Spirit to a royal seal, authenticating our faith, declaring God's ownership, and placing us under his inviolable protection.
- The Spirit is also a down-payment on the future kingdom: his presence inside us is God's pledge that the full inheritance is coming.
- This inward gift replaces mere law-keeping with heart-level transformation, fixing our "broken choosers" so we begin to desire and do what pleases God.
- Spiritual growth rests on trusting the Spirit's transforming power rather than mastering techniques or summoning a controllable "force."
- The Spirit distributes a rich diversity of roles and opportunities to build up Christ's unified body.

- Our task is to watch for opportunities, employ whatever talents or resources God has provided, and trust the Spirit to weave our varied contributions into his greater kingdom design.

See for Yourself

Ephesians 1:13–23; John 3:1–13; 1 Corinthians 12; Acts 2:1–4

Reflection

Where have you noticed a practical need in your church, workplace, neighborhood, or circle of friends, and what first step could you take to help fill it?

14

HOPE

HOLDING ON UNTIL THE END

Ask, and it will be given to you; seek, and you will find;
knock, and it will be opened to you.

— MATTHEW 7:7

J esus made an incredible promise. He assured us that when
we ask, God gives; when we seek, we find; and when we
knock, the door opens (Matthew 7:7). But if we're honest,
many of us sometimes wonder: *Will it work?*

At some level, the gospel feels too good to be true. Thankfully, Jesus knew we would wrestle with that question, and he
spoke directly to that doubt.

At first glance, his words seem simple: ask God for something and he'll give it to you. What could be better than that?
After all, good parents delight in giving good gifts to their children. God is far better than any earthly parent because he is
perfectly good. His generosity isn't mixed with pride, impatience, or selfishness. It flows from a character that is pure, holy,
and full of love.

But then you might think, *Wait a minute. God doesn't always say yes. Sometimes the answer is no.* Sometimes when you knock, the door remains closed. Any good parent says no when it's wise and necessary. So what does Jesus mean? How does this promise work?

To make sense of it, let's revisit the four core convictions of R.E.A.L. faith. These truths help us to see Jesus' words in context and remind us that God keeps his promises to those who seek him.

CONVICTION 1: RECOGNIZE YOUR SIN

The first core conviction of saving faith is the recognition that, because of our sin, we deserve judgment, not blessings. Not only does God owe us nothing, he would be within his rights to condemn us for our rebellion.

When Jesus says that God gives excellent gifts, he doesn't mean that we have somehow earned God's favor. He means that God, in his mercy, gives grace instead of judgment.

If we approach God demanding what we think we've earned, we'll receive exactly what sin earns: condemnation. But if we come to God humbly, confessing our sin and asking for mercy, Jesus promises God will respond with grace and forgiveness. We may deserve condemnation, but Jesus assures us that God delights in giving good gifts to those who ask in faith.

CONVICTION 2: EMBRACE YOUR NEED

The second core conviction of R.E.A.L. faith is understanding that God is not obligated to give us anything: not comfort, not answers, not even the next breath. He gives us gifts because he delights in giving. He answers prayer because he is loving and kind, just like any good father who cares deeply for his children.

Jesus' promise applies to those who come to God in humility with saving faith. People who approach God with a sense of entitlement, assuming that God must give them what they want, will find the door closed. But for those who trust him, Jesus offers something remarkable: even though God owes us nothing, he joyfully gives good gifts to those who ask.

CONVICTION 3: ACCEPT GOD'S GRACE

Saving faith longs for holiness and freedom from sin. But it's easy to lose sight of the fact that freedom from sin is the gift we need most. We get so distracted by the cares and pleasures of this world that we forget what truly matters. So God's good gifts aren't always what we expect.

When Jesus says, "ask, seek, and knock," he's not promising that God will grant every wish like a genie. He's promising that God will always give us what we truly need: freedom from sin, forgiveness, wisdom, and a place in his kingdom.

For example, if you pray, *God, don't let people dislike me for following you,* the answer will be no. Jesus warned that people will hate you because you follow him.

Or if you ask, *God, let me ignore my sin so I don't feel guilty,* the answer will also be no. God loves you too much to leave you in spiritual darkness.

But if you pray, *Father, forgive me and give me the good things you promise,* you will receive. Every believer prays this request in some form, and God always says yes.

If you wonder if God will really forgive you, the answer is an emphatic yes. Seek forgiveness, and you will find it. Knock on the door to the kingdom of heaven, and it will open. You can count on it. Jesus has excellent news for those who seek what God says is truly valuable. He assures us that God gives what is truly valuable to those who ask.

FAITH KEEPS ASKING

Asking, seeking, and knocking are expressions of faith. We desperately need what God has promised: mercy, wisdom, and rescue from sin and death. But God doesn't give these gifts automatically to every human being simply because we're human. We must respond to the gospel by believing and seeking to live as if it is true.

Imagine you are a street-tough, angry kid who has been adopted by a patient, compassionate father. On your first day in your new home, he tells you, "I know you've lived a hard life. But you're not alone anymore. I'll help you finish school, kick your worst habits, and build a new kind of life. All you have to do is ask."

But you're not convinced. His promises sound too good to be true, and deep down, you are not sure you really trust him. So you start with impossible requests, daring him to fail you. He calmly says no, without anger or judgment.

Next, you fall back on what you know: manipulation, half-truths, and charm when it suits you. But it doesn't feel the same anymore. The old survival tricks leave a bitter taste, and a voice in the back of your mind whispers, *Father would be disappointed if he knew.*

Eventually, you take a chance. You ask for something small but real. And he helps, no lecture, no strings. So you ask again, this time for something bigger. Sometimes the answer is yes. Sometimes the answer is no, because he knows what you really need. But now you keep asking, not to test him, but because you believe he loves you.

The fact that you keep coming back regardless of the answer says something important about your relationship with your father. It shows you trust him.

This story illustrates how we should think of prayer and

doubt. Faith is not the absence of doubt, but the choice to keep coming back.

Some people think that faith means never having doubts. They think that if you have questions or ever struggle to believe, your faith must not be genuine. But that's not true. Even the strongest believers wrestle with doubt.

Doubt isn't the opposite of faith; it's part of the journey. Saving faith doesn't mean that you never waver. It means that you keep turning back to God when you do. You keep asking and knocking, knowing that Jesus promises that those who seek will find.

Life in this broken world is hard and difficult. Every day we face temptations and trials that test our faith and make us choose between God's way or the world's way. Some days, believing God's promises feels anything but easy. Sometimes we choose well. At other times, we fail and repent. But in both situations, we persevere in believing in God's promises, even when believing is difficult.

Normal daily life confronts us with important questions: *Do I really believe the gospel? Do I trust God? Do I truly want what he has promised?*

The life of faith involves clinging to those truths, and holding fast when it would be easier to let go. And in that struggle, we turn to our Father in prayer. We ask, seek, and knock again and again.

Our calling on this side of heaven is to hold fast to God's promises, and to keep trusting him, all the way to the end. The prayer Jesus describes, the one that asks, seeks, and knocks, is a prayer of faith.

And when your grip feels weak, Jesus offers incredibly good news: Ask for faith, and God will give it. Seek forgiveness, and you will find it. Knock on the door of heaven, and it will open. God promises eternal life to those who keep seeking him.

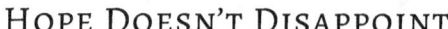

HOPE DOESN'T DISAPPOINT

Sometimes, it feels like our prayers disappear into silence because the waiting is long and the answers seem slow. In those times, Scripture urges us to pray and not lose heart. God promises that he will never lose any of his children (John 10:28–29). Or as Paul puts it: our hope in Christ will not put us to shame (Romans 5:5).

In English, we often use the word hope to express uncertainty. We'd like something to happen, but don't know if it will. Biblical hope is different. In the New Testament, hope never refers to wishful thinking, such as "I hope it doesn't rain tonight."

Hope is not a vague desire or a shot in the dark.

Hope is the confident, eager expectation that something good is coming.

Like a child counting down the days until Christmas, hope is anchored in fact. It looks forward with confident joy because it's based on the promises of a faithful God.

Believers are not hoping for Christmas though. We are hoping for the glory of God. Glory can sound abstract, but think of it like this: When something is glorious, it captivates us. It grabs our attention and fills us with wonder.

A brilliant sunset, a breathtaking mountain view, and a bright shining light in the darkness have a glorious quality that demands our attention and awe. God's glory captures us like that. He is holy, powerful, loving, merciful, and just. His character commands our awe and respect.

One day, God will share one aspect of his glory with us: he

will make us holy as he is holy. He will free us from sin and make us morally beautiful, worthy, and perfect. When he removes sin forever, we will finally experience life as he meant it to be: untouched by corruption, futility, and death. That's our future. That's the hope of the glory of God that we're holding onto.

Now, you might think: *Rejoicing in the hope of God's glory sounds wonderful, but it only applies if I'm really a believer. What if one day I walk away and go back to my old life?*

You are not alone in that fear. The New Testament authors expected believers would wrestle with doubt, especially when life gets hard. As we saw, one way we know we have genuine saving faith is that our faith perseveres through trials.

But Paul gives us another reason: Our faith won't fail us because God loves us (Romans 5:1–11).

THE GREATER LOVE

Imagine you're playing catch in the front yard with your little sister. Suddenly, the ball gets away from her, and she goes running after it, right into the path of an oncoming car.

You don't hesitate. You dash in front of the car, yelling for her to move and for the car to stop. Thankfully, you scoop your sister into your arms just as the car skids to a stop.

Now imagine this scenario again. This time the person in front of the car is the older kid who bullies you in school. He made your life miserable for the entire school year.

Would you attempt to run in front of the car to save him? Probably not. But if you pushed him out of harm's way, how much love would that take compared to saving your sister? Which is a greater demonstration of love: to die for your sister or to die for your enemy?

Let's go one step further. Imagine that you muster the courage to run in front of that car for your enemy. As you do, he laughs at you and mocks you. Even as you save his life, he tells you that you're a fool for trying.

Wouldn't that take greater love still? God has already showed that kind of love.

Jesus died for us while we were his enemies.

God sent Jesus to die for us while we were like that mocking bully in front of the car. Now that you're his child, do you think he will hesitate to scoop you into his arms when you stumble? He's already done the harder act of love: dying for you when you were his enemy. Why would he abandon you now that you are part of his family?

SANCTIFICATION SECURE

But there's more good news: you can't mess this up. You can't resist, delay, or derail God's plan. Many new believers mistakenly think that God has done his part and now the rest is up to us. They think our job is to learn to be "better" Christians, and muster up mature saving faith.

Your sanctification does not depend on praying the right way or trying harder. You cannot hinder, stop, or thwart the Holy Spirit. Remember, he blows through your life like the wind to bring about God's plan for you.

You can be sure you'll persevere in faith, not because you're strong, but because God loves you. The cross showed how far God would go to save you. Having died on the cross for you, Jesus will not let you go now.

Somewhere along the line, many of us absorbed the idea that "God helps those who help themselves." But that's not the gospel, and it's not in the Bible.

A more accurate proverb is: God helps those who know they can't help themselves. He doesn't reward the self-sufficient. He answers those who ask, seek, and knock. Saving faith isn't a power move. It's dependence on the One who can save us and it keeps asking, seeking and knocking.

Does Christianity work? Absolutely. God has demonstrated that he loves us enough to keep his promises. You can have complete confidence. Not only will you make it through tomorrow and the tribulations ahead, you'll cross the finish line and receive eternal life in the kingdom of God, because God loves you and he will never let you go.

Summary

- Asking, seeking, and knocking are part of faith. We keep turning to God because we trust him, even when the waiting is long or hard.
- Biblical hope is a confident, joyful expectation that God will keep his promises.
- Enduring trials is evidence of saving faith.
- Hope will not disappoint, because God has demonstrated he loves us enough to ensure we find eternal life.

See for Yourself

Romans 5:1–11; Matthew 7:7–11; 1 Peter 1:1–13; Romans 8:12–25

Reflection

Do you struggle to believe God will answer your prayers? Why or why not?

15

EIGHT TRUTHS TO REMEMBER

Therefore, my brothers, whom I love and long for, my joy and crown, stand firm thus in the Lord, my beloved.

— PHILIPPIANS 4:1

In the introduction, I compared following Jesus to stepping into the middle of a movie without knowing the plot. Now, as we come to this final chapter, you've seen enough of the story to recognize the main characters, follow the action, and know where all of this is headed.

You have learned:

- the gospel is a Copernican worldview shift that transforms your life;
- what we're being saved from (sin);
- where we're headed (holiness);
- how we're saved (the cross and four convictions of saving faith);
- how we grow in faith (trials and the work of the Spirit);

148

• the confident hope that anchors us (ask, seek, knock).

But this isn't the closing scene. It's the moment you step into your role. As the story shifts from understanding to action, there's a right way and a wrong way to apply this knowledge. First, the wrong way.

CUT THE RED WIRE

Imagine you're in a superhero movie. The villain has planted a bomb, and the fate of the world rests in your hands. The timer ticks away. You stare at a tangled mess of colored wires, trying to decide which one to cut.

Just as panic rises, your sidekick spots a small booklet tucked into the frame.

"Wait," he says, tugging it free. "I think this is the manual."

It's written in an alien language, of course, but like most instruction booklets, it's mostly pictures. On page ten, there's an image of scissors cutting a red wire. That's it. You cut the red wire and save the day.

Some people treat the gospel like that bomb manual. They view it as a set of instructions to follow so you can be saved: believe in Jesus, confess your sins, join a church, pray, be nice. Do the list, and you go to heaven.

But that's not the best way to understand the gospel. In fact, you may have noticed, I haven't given you any steps for how to do Christianity right.

Let me offer a different way to think about how the gospel worldview transforms your life.

THE QUEST

Picture a fairy tale instead. A prince falls in love with a beautiful princess but, alas, she is enchanted. Her fairy godmother explains that he must succeed in three quests to break the spell and win her heart.

First, he must bring back a jewel guarded by a fierce dragon. Next, he must trek through the desert and solve a tricky riddle from a Sphinx. Finally, he must convince a wise prophet on a tall mountain that he's the smartest man around.

You could say that the prince has all the information he needs to succeed. He knows the three tasks he must accomplish to free his love, win her heart, and live happily ever after. But the instructions tell him only what must be done. They don't tell him how to do it.

These aren't step-by-step instructions like "cut the red wire." They require him to be the right kind of person to succeed. If he cares more about himself than her, he won't go near a dragon, let alone cross a desert or climb a mountain. To succeed, he needs to be a person of courage, wisdom, and commitment. Without those character traits, he doesn't stand a chance.

How did the prince wrest the jewel away from the dragon? Well, unlike everyone else who charged in with their swords and got burned to a crisp, the prince showed kindness to the dragon. He offered to trade one of his kingdom's treasures for the jewel. The dragon agreed.

How did he solve the riddle of the Sphinx? He didn't rush or guess. He used his critical thinking skills and kept digging until he found the right answer.

How did he prove himself to be the wisest man of all? Because he had read about Socrates, he admitted that he didn't know all the answers.

The instructions didn't make him kind, clever, or humble. They gave him a chance to become kind, clever, and humble. The gospel works like that too. It's not a checklist. It's an invitation to discover who you are and to let God transform you from the inside out.

The Gospel Worldview

The Christian life is not about following rules to earn God's love. It is not a set of tasks to accomplish, behaviors to adopt, or answers to memorize. It's a Copernican shift in worldview that changes your life.

Like the prince in the fairy tale, as we face choices, temptations, and trials, we reveal our fundamental beliefs. The gospel doesn't teach us how to cut the red wires of life so we can be better people.

Rather, because of the cross, God shows us mercy and gives us his Spirit so that we can see the truth. As the Spirit opens our eyes, the truths of the Bible begin to make sense and we increasingly become people who value what God values. Like the prince in the fairy tale, our life choices reveal the faith God is growing in us.

That's how lasting change begins. The Spirit teaches us truth, and that truth reshapes how we see the world and how we live in it. We won't get everything right, but we begin making different choices, not to earn God's love, but because we trust him.

With the foundation laid, we can now distill the Christian worldview into eight core truths.

Truth #1: The God of the Bible is real.

Most people are not atheists. They believe in some kind of spiritual force or higher power. But we lie to ourselves about who that higher power is. We ignore the God who created everything and revealed himself in Scripture. Instead, we invent a god who fits our preferences.

But when we come to know the God who sent the prophets, the apostles, and Jesus, our worldview begins to shift. He is good and merciful. He keeps his promises and offers us salvation through Jesus Christ. That's where faith begins.

TRUTH #2: GOD'S THE CENTER, NOT US.

God is at the center of the universe, and we are not. You and I stand as equals before him. Before conversion, we all think our needs matter more than anyone else's. We walk into most situations asking: *What's in it for me?*

The Spirit changes that selfish perspective. He shows us that God made every human being in his image and that makes us equal. No one is better than anyone else. The shift from self-centeredness to seeing others as fellow image-bearers transforms how we treat the people around us.

TRUTH #3: WE ARE GUILTY SINNERS.

At our core, we are all selfish and we are guilty before God. One day, we will face his judgment, and he has every right to condemn us. But God offers mercy, not because we've earned it, but because he chooses to be merciful.

That truth shifts how we see other people. When you understand we are all guilty, you stop expecting perfection from others. You stop judging them. They need God's mercy just as much as you do.

TRUTH #4: GOD IS AT WORK IN YOUR LIFE.

Even though we're sinners, God shows us mercy and forgiveness through Jesus. But he doesn't stop there. He is active in our lives, shaping us for good. He's healing what's broken and strengthening what's weak.

That truth gives you something solid to stand on when life

gets hard. Your life isn't spinning out of control. God has a plan and a purpose, and that purpose is good.

The more you trust that God is taking care of you, the more free you are to love others. You don't need to demand your fair share or fight to be right. You can be generous, kind, and forgiving, because God's got it all under control.

TRUTH #5: TRUSTING GOD GIVES US HOPE.

Knowing that God is in control of everything gives us hope. Guilt, death, sin, and futility are overwhelming. None of us can solve these problems. But God can and he promised he will. Then he proved it by resurrecting Jesus.

That promise gives us a solid foundation and a confident expectation: our eternal destiny is secure. Nothing in our lives is random. God weaves everything into his plan to bring us to that good and glorious end. Our lives aren't careening out of control. They have meaning and purpose. And they're headed toward a joyful, lasting home.

The more we grasp the hope of the gospel, the more we delight in God's promises. It doesn't make life painless, but it makes life hopeful. God promises exactly what we need. And that gives us a joyful confidence. We can stay grounded in a topsy-turvy world because we're standing on the solid rock of truth and our destiny is secure.

TRUTH #6: WE ARE CONNECTED TO OTHER BELIEVERS.

Your hope in the gospel links you to other followers of Jesus. You may differ greatly from them, but you share the same faith and the same goal, and that's the deepest kind of bond. You're part of the same family. You're on the same journey. And you'll spend eternity together.

TRUTH #7: HOPE SETS US FREE.

When you trust God is in charge, you don't have to fight for everything right now. You can be patient and forgiving, even when others hurt you, because God will make things right in the end. You don't have to demand your share or chase down justice on your own. God is weaving your life into his greater story. That kind of hope brings freedom. It allows you to rest, to wait, and to trust him.

TRUTH #8: SAVING FAITH MAKES US LOVE WHAT IS RIGHT AND GOOD.

The world tells us that goodness is limiting and that God's boundaries keep us from living life to the fullest. But the gospel helps us see the truth that following God is the only path to life. His boundaries don't hold us back; they protect us. God is fixing what's broken and leading us toward what's better. The way to eternal life is to walk with him.

FINISH STRONG

The gospel isn't about cutting the right wire to avoid disaster. It's about becoming the kind of person who follows God because you trust him completely. It's not about earning God's love. It's about receiving the love he's already given you.

So take hold of these truths. Let them reshape how you see the world. Strive to live your life in the light of these truths. Honor God in the way you handle sexuality, work, and money. And you will not only start strong in your journey of faith, you'll finish strong.

This is just the foundation. Keep asking questions. Keep seeking truth. Keep turning to Scripture. You're not alone, and you're not done. You've started strong. By God's grace, you'll finish strong too.

SEE FOR YOURSELF

Colossians 1:13–23 (Truth #2); Romans 3:1–31 (Truth #3); Isaiah 40:12–31 (Truth #4 & #5); Romans 5:1–11 (Truth #5 & #7); Ephesians 4:11–16 (Truth #6); Galatians 5:16–26 (Truth #8)

REFLECTION

What did you learn that challenged you most? Encouraged you most? Surprised you most? What do you most want to remember and pray about? What do you want to learn next?

A NOTE AT THE END

PLEASE REVIEW THIS BOOK!

Reviews help authors more than you think! If you were blessed by this book, please write a review on Amazon. Even if it's only a line or two, I would greatly appreciate it.

Scan this code to leave a review on Amazon:

And please tell a friend about *Start Strong*. A book in the right hands at the right time can change a life.

Keep Learning

Wednesday in the Word is my podcast about what the Bible means and how we know. Each season covers a book of the Bible or a topical study. It's the same clear, thoughtful, and biblically grounded approach you've seen here, just in audio form.

Subscribe wherever you listen to your podcasts or visit WednesdayintheWord.com to listen and learn more.

READER AND LEADER EXTRAS

Whether you're reading on your own or leading a group, these tools are here to serve you.

All resources at krisan.com/startstrongbonus

Start Strong: A New Believer's Podcast: Each episode unpacks a key Bible passage from the "See for Yourself" list, explained clearly, applied practically. Build your faith with real understanding. Listen free on the *Wednesday in the Word with Krisan Marotta* podcast.

∼

Companion Workbook: The companion workbook helps you slow down, reflect, and remember what you're learning in *Start Strong*. With guided questions, journal prompts, and space to capture your own insights, it turns ideas into application.

∼

Free Discussion Questions: These questions help you reflect more deeply, spark meaningful conversation, and apply what you're learning to real life. Ideal for book clubs, small groups, mentoring, and discipling.

Free Leader Lesson Plans: This chapter-by-chapter guide is built for teaching, discussing, and applying the Scripture behind *Start Strong* in any classroom setting. Each plan includes Scripture, key themes, and open-ended questions.

Quizzes for Youth & Homeschoolers: Two quick, multiple-choice comprehension quizzes—one for Middle Grades (6–8) and one for High School (9–12)—to help students review what they've learned from *Start Strong* and identify what they might want to revisit.

Bulk Buying Discounts: If you're ordering for a church, campus ministry, homeschool co-op, or class, contact me and I'll help you figure out the best way to order for your group.

ACKNOWLEDGMENTS

Thanks to my first and best editor, my best friend, the first person who suggested I teach the Bible—my husband, David John Marotta. I would never have dared to teach the Bible, start a podcast, or write this book without your support and encouragement.

I'm deeply grateful to all my mentors who shaped my understanding of Scripture and modeled what it means to love God with all your heart, soul, mind, and strength. You laid the foundation this book stands on.

I am especially grateful to Jack Crabtree who first walked me through the book of Romans, taught me the four convictions of saving faith, and continually challenges me to be a better student of the Word.

I'm also grateful to the late Ron Julian whose illustrations have stayed with me for decades and now appear in these pages: Copernicus (chapter 5), the kids on the playground (chapter 5), fearing the king (chapter 6), and the quest (chapter 12).

Thanks to my friend Margaret Sholaas for the million pennies analogy (chapter 2).

A heartfelt thank you to Matheson Russell for his thoughtful proofreading and careful attention to detail. Your generous help strengthened this book in ways that truly matter.

Thanks go to my diligent, and faithful beta readers: Kathryn Anderson-Uhrik, John Hughes, Charles Johnson, Lauren Lockhart, Frank McGraw, Kathy Stone, and Beverly Winchester. Your feedback helped shape the final manuscript in ways I couldn't have done alone.

To my incredible street team: Anne McCain Brown, Martha Carroll, Sara Dickinson, Nancy Cummings, Kathi Gibson, Homer Hickam, Linda Howard, Susan Jones, Lauren Lockhart, Sue Manning, Paul Marotta, Roland Maurice, Cannie Mawson, Ruth Scully, Ruth Martha Scully, Melissa Stella, Lia Thoms-Price, Pam van der Linde, and Christi Wildman. Thank you for showing up, spreading the word, and cheering me on. Your support helped bring this book into the world, and I'm deeply grateful.

Most of all, thanks to the Lord Jesus Christ, who saved me, taught me, and gave me a love for his Word I could never keep to myself.

GLOSSARY

Abraham: Old Testament patriarch God called to leave his homeland and trust God for a new nation; honored as the father of the Jewish nation and the "father of the faith" (Genesis 12).

Adoption: Legal picture of God welcoming believers as his children, giving them an inheritance in his eternal kingdom (Ephesians 1:5).

Armor of God: A metaphor used by the apostle Paul (Ephesians 6) to describe the spiritual preparation believers need to stand firm in their faith.

Ask, Seek, Knock: Expressions of persistent faith in prayer, as taught by Jesus. This practice signifies a lifelong trust in God, who promises to give believers what they truly need: forgiveness, wisdom, holiness, and eternal life. It demonstrates an ongoing belief and dependence on God's faithfulness.

Atoning Sacrifice / Atonement: A legal and theological term meaning to make amends or compensate for a wrong. It refers to Jesus Christ's death on the cross, which fully paid the debt for humanity's sin, satisfying God's justice and clearing the way for forgiveness.

Augustine of Hippo: 4th century North African bishop whose *Confessions* and *City of God* still shape Christian thinking on grace and human nature.

Baptism: Outward sign of identifying with Jesus' death and resurrection, being dipped under water to symbolize dying to sin and being raised to new life.

Born Again / New Birth: A metaphor for the spiritual transformation initiated by God's Holy Spirit, essential for entering the kingdom of God. This divine intervention changes a person from the inside, making them part of God's family and instilling new desires for holiness. It is not achieved through human effort or willpower but is a gift from God.

Broken Chooser: The author's term for the inner faculty of a human being (heart, will, soul, or nature) that determines desires, priorities, and actions. Due to the Fall (sin's entry into the world), this "chooser" is broken, leading humanity to inherently act from selfish motives, underscoring the need for divine transformation.

Chastity: A specific aspect of God's design for sexuality, referring to sexual purity before marriage. It represents a conscious choice to honor God's intended purpose for intimacy.

Confess Jesus is Lord: The central declaration and defining mark of a genuine believer. It means acknowledging Jesus' authority to forgive sins and grant eternal life, and committing to follow his teachings and commands.

Copernican Shift: The author's metaphor illustrating the profound transformation in a believer's worldview, akin to Nicolaus Copernicus' discovery that the earth orbits the sun. Spiritually, it means realizing that God is the true center of the universe, and human beings are equal before him.

Copernicus, Nicolaus: 16th century astronomer whose sun-centered model illustrates the "Copernican shift" of putting God, not self, at the center.

Covenant: Binding promise-relationship God initiates with his people; the "new covenant" Jesus sealed by his blood guarantees forgiveness and a heart empowered to obey (Jeremiah 31:31–34; Luke 22:20).There are two kinds of covenants in Scripture: unilateral and bilateral. **Unilateral:** A commitment on the part of a greater party to a lesser. The majority of covenants in the Bible are this type. **Bilateral:** A commitment on the part of two equals to fulfill certain promises unconditionally (e.g. marriage).

The Cross: The pivotal event in human history, where Jesus willingly bore humanity's sin and punishment. The cross is the unique meeting point of God's perfect justice and boundless mercy, where Jesus' death paid the staggering debt owed by sinners, thereby enabling their forgiveness and reconciliation with God.

David (King): Old Testament shepherd who became the second King of Israel, whose life showed passionate devotion to God, despite serious failures.

Death (biblical sense): A comprehensive consequence of sin, extending beyond mere physical cessation of life. Death includes spiritual separation from God, the pervasive principle of entropy (decay and unraveling of all good), futility, and corruption that affects all creation and human relationships.

Disciple/Follower of Jesus: An individual who has decided to trust in the cross of Jesus Christ and seek to live by his teachings.

Doubt: An acknowledged, natural component of the faith journey, not necessarily antithetical to genuine belief. Saving faith is characterized by persistently turning back to God, asking, seeking, and knocking, even amidst wavering, trusting in Jesus' promises.

Entropy: A scientific principle measuring the level of disorder in a system, which illustrates sin's pervasive effect on creation. Entropy describes the universal tendency towards disorder, decay, and corruption. Sin causes everything physical, relational, and moral to unravel and fall apart unless divine intervention occurs.

Equality (biblical sense): A foundational truth that all human beings are made in God's image, regardless of their circumstances, talents, or social status. This means everyone is equally broken by sin, equally valuable to God, and equally in need of his grace, prompting believers to treat others without favoritism or judgment.

Eternal Life: More than just unending existence, it signifies a life characterized by holiness, flourishing, and complete freedom from the effects of sin, death, decay, futility, and corruption. It is the promised state in the coming kingdom of heaven, where believers will be fully restored and made holy.

Faith (Saving Faith): An ongoing, personal, and life-changing trust in Jesus Christ as the sole hope for salvation. It is a gift from God, and demonstrated by a life that increasingly aligns with God's will and truth, as outlined by the R.E.A.L. acronym.

The Fall: The pivotal moment recorded in Genesis 3 when the first humans, Adam and Eve, rebelled against God. This rebellion introduced sin, death, and corruption into the world, fundamentally altering humanity's nature and leading to inherent sinfulness and guilt before a holy God.

Fear God: A foundational principle of wisdom in the Christian life. It involves taking God more seriously than anything else, allowing his opinion and commands to weigh most heavily in decisions. It is not a paralyzing dread but a profound allegiance, awe, and respect balanced with trust in his kindness and mercy.

Fidelity: A specific aspect of God's design for sexuality, referring to sexual faithfulness within marriage. It is a commitment to one's spouse within the covenant of marriage, upholding sexual integrity and honoring God's intended purpose for intimacy.

Glory of God: God's inherent, captivating character, encompassing his holiness, power, love, mercy, and justice, which demands awe and respect. Biblical hope for believers includes the confident expectation of one day reflecting this glory, specifically by being made holy and morally perfect like God.

Golden Rule: Jesus' command to "as you wish that others would do to you, do so to them" (Luke 6:31). This precept reflects God's design for human interaction, stemming from the understanding that all people are equally created in God's image and are equally in need of grace and mercy, prompting believers to act with compassion.

Gospel: Meaning "good news," it is the core message of Christianity: that humanity is guilty due to sin, but through his death and resurrection, Jesus Christ provides rescue and justification.

Gospel Worldview: The transformative way of viewing and understanding the world that results from believing the gospel. It involves a fundamental "Copernican shift" where God, not self, becomes the center of one's understanding of reality, profoundly influencing values, desires, and actions.

Grace: The unmerited favor and undeserved gift of God. Salvation is entirely a gift of grace, as God chose to accept Jesus' atoning sacrifice on humanity's behalf, despite humanity's unworthiness and rebellion.

Guilt: An objective debt before God, resulting from humanity's rebellion against him. Guilt is based on truth and demands justice. It cannot be erased by apologies or self-effort, requiring divine intervention through justification.

Heart: The inner faculty of a person that determines desires, priorities, and actions. Because of the Fall, humanity's "chooser" is broken, leading to sin and making it impossible to become perfect through willpower alone. The Holy Spirit begins fixing this brokenness in believers.

Holiness: A core attribute of God and a state to which believers are called. It means being set apart for God's purposes and progressively conforming to his moral character, which is pure and without sin.

Holy Spirit: The third person of the Trinity, sent by God to transform believers after Jesus' ascension. He acts as a seal of authenticity, ownership, and protection, guaranteeing the believer's future inheritance and completion of salvation.

Hope (biblical sense): A confident, joyful expectation of something known is coming, anchored in trust in God's promises. For believers, this hope is specifically the hope of the glory of God, anticipating a future where they will be made holy and experience eternal life.

Image of God / Imago Dei: Truth that every person reflects God's character and value, grounding human dignity and equality (Genesis 1:27).

Individual Work of the Spirit / Spiritual Gifts: Diverse roles and opportunities that God gives to believers. These gifts are meant for service, building up the church, and reflecting God's varied grace in practical ways.

Isaac: Promised son of Abraham and Sarah, through whom God continued the covenant line. (Genesis 21).

James: New Testament apostle and author, often seen as in conflict with the apostle Paul.

Jeremiah: Old Testament prophet who foretold God writing his law on human hearts.

Jesus Christ: The Messiah. God's Son whose life, death, and resurrection provide salvation. The second person of the Trinity.

Job: Old Testament man tested by intense suffering yet commended for enduring faith.

Joel: Old Testament prophet who envisioned God's Spirit poured out on all people.

John, the Apostle: Follower of Jesus and author of one of the four gospels.

Journey of Faith: A central metaphor for the Christian life describing the process of believing, growing, and living as a follower of Jesus, with the goal to persevere in faith.

Justification: God's legal act of declaring a sinner innocent or righteous solely on the basis of Jesus Christ's work on the cross. Through justification, a believer's guilt is removed, their record is cleared, and their relationship with God is restored.

Kingdom of Heaven: The future, perfected realm where Jesus reigns and everything broken by sin is made new. When Jesus returns, death, decay, and moral ruin will be reversed, and all creation will flourish under his just and righteous rule.

Law (biblical sense): God's commands that reveal his character and our need for grace, summarized in the Ten Commandments and recorded in the Old Testament.

Living Quietly: A principle for Christian life and work, urging believers to live faithfully within the specific calling God has given them, without striving for external recognition or impact. It involves diligently caring for one's responsibilities, minding one's own business, and trusting God with the outcomes.

Love (biblical sense): Defined primarily by action rather than emotion or words. It means acting for the good of another person, modeled after God's sacrificial love in sending Jesus. For believers, it's a natural outflow of a God-centered worldview, extending to both God and neighbor.

Lydia: First recorded European convert, a businesswoman whose home hosted early believers (Acts 16).

Maturity (spiritual): The process of growing in wisdom and faith, often through trials. It is not perfection but involves increasing humility, quicker repentance, and a deeper confidence in God's faithfulness, equipping believers to endure and trust God more profoundly.

Mediator (biblical sense): Jesus' essential role in bridging the gap between God and sinful humanity. As mediator, Jesus reconciled the estranged parties by satisfying the demands of God's justice through his atoning sacrifice on the cross, thereby enabling forgiveness and the restoration of the relationship between God and his people.

Mercy: God's compassionate response to humanity's sinful state, where he chooses not to give us the condemnation we deserve.

Moses: Old Testament prophet and leader who delivered Israel from Egypt and longed for God's Spirit on all people.

New Commandment (Jesus): Jesus' teaching to his disciples that they love one another (John 13:34–35). This mutual love among believers is the distinguishing mark by which the world recognizes followers of Jesus.

Nicodemus: First century Pharisee who sought Jesus at night and learned about being born again (John 3).

Noah: Old Testament patriarch whom God told to build an ark; by trusting God and riding out the great flood, he became the ancestor of every post-flood nation (Genesis 6).

Paul, the Apostle: Former persecutor turned follower of Jesus whose letters form most of the New Testament.

Peter, the Apostle: The apostle who denied Jesus yet became a bold leader after the resurrection.

Pentecost: The day when the Holy Spirit dramatically descended upon the apostles of Jesus in Jerusalem (Acts 2), fulfilling Old Testament prophecies.

Perseverance (Steadfastness): Spiritual resilience developed through tested faith, enabling believers to remain firm and rooted in Christ despite life's challenges. Endurance proves the authenticity of saving faith and contributes to spiritual maturity and wholeness.

Persevere in Faith: The lifelong mission for believers to cling steadfastly to Jesus and the gospel truth until the end.

R.E.A.L. Faith: The author's acronym defining the four core convictions of saving faith: Recognize sin; Embrace need; Accept grace; Lean on Jesus. This framework is a shorthand for the four core convictions of saving faith.

Ransom: A term describing Jesus' death as a payment required to set humanity free from slavery to sin and the condemnation of guilt. Like a payment for a slave or prisoner of war, Jesus' sacrifice paid the price to redeem believers, highlighting the legal and redemptive nature of his work (Mark 10:45).

Reconciliation: Restored friendship between God and people once hostile to him, accomplished when Jesus satisfied justice.

Redemption: Act of God buying his people back from slavery to sin at the cost of Jesus' blood, like paying a ransom to set captives free.

Repentance: A foundational act in the faith journey, signifying a complete change of direction. It involves turning away from sin and decisively reorienting one's heart and mind towards God. It is more than guilt or regret; it is a shift in allegiance and a longing for holiness.

Resurrection: Historical event where Jesus physically rose from the dead, proving his victory over sin and guaranteeing believers' eternal life.

Sanctification: The will of God for believers; it is the daily, lifelong process of becoming holy and more like God. It involves being set apart for God's purposes and progressively conforming to his moral character, living out one's new identity as someone who belongs to God.

Sarah: Wife of Abraham who bore Isaac in her old age (Genesis 17).

Satisfaction: A theological concept describing how Jesus Christ's sacrifice on the cross fully met the demands of God's justice for humanity's sin. By his death, Jesus satisfied justice on believers' behalf.

Saving Faith: An ongoing, personal trust in Jesus Christ as one's only hope for salvation. Saving faith is a gift from God. It is characterized by the R.E.A.L. convictions (Recognize Sin, Embrace Need, Accept Grace, Lean on Jesus).

Seal (of the Spirit): An image drawn from ancient royal practice of using a seal to authenticate documents. It signifies authenticity, ownership, and protection. When God seals believers with his Holy Spirit, it proves their faith is genuine, marks them as his own, and assures them of his protection and preservation for eternity.

Sexual Immorality: Any sexual behavior that deviates from God's intended design. God intended sexuality to be enjoyed within marriage, which is a lifelong, monogamous union between one man and one woman.

Sexual Integrity: A life characterized by honesty, dignity, and purity in sexual choices. It involves conducting oneself openly before God and others, avoiding actions that cause shame, regret, or harm. It is about honoring God's design for sexuality and valuing others rightly, as opposed to pursuing "passion of lust" (1 Thessalonians 4:5).

Sin: The central problem addressed by the Bible, sin is a posture of the heart that says 'no' to God and 'yes' to self. It distorts perception, leads to death (entropy, decay), and incurs guilt before a holy God, permeating every part of human nature.

Spiritual Gifts: Unique roles, opportunities, and abilities distributed by the Holy Spirit to believers for the good of the whole body of Christ (1 Corinthians 12–14). These are opportunities for service and promote unity in diversity within the church.

Substitution: A key aspect of Jesus' atoning sacrifice, meaning that Jesus took the punishment for humanity's sin. Though innocent, he bore the penalty that sinners deserved, allowing them to be declared free and justified before God, emphasizing the legal nature of his sacrifice.

Total Depravity: A theological concept affirming that sin has affected every part of human nature, thoughts, motives, desires, and actions. It means no part of a person remains untainted by sin, making self-salvation impossible.

Trials: Any form of hardship, difficulty, or challenge that tests a believer's trust in God. Trials are an integral part of God's plan to refine, strengthen, and prove the authenticity of faith, leading to spiritual maturity.

The Trinity: Christian doctrine that the one true God eternally exists as three Persons—Father, Son, and Holy Spirit—equal in deity, united in love.

Two Greatest Commandments: Jesus' summary of the Law and the Prophets: "You shall love the Lord your God with all your heart and with all your soul and with all your mind. . . And a second is like it: You shall love your neighbor as yourself" (Matthew 22:37–40). These naturally flow from recognizing God at the center.

Universal Work of the Spirit: The Holy Spirit's foundational work of giving saving faith to every believer. This work enables a person to see and understand the truth of the gospel, without which no one could be saved, distinguishing it from individual spiritual gifts.

Vocation / Calling: The unique, God-given purpose and set of responsibilities for each individual's life. This includes not just paid employment but also roles in family, community, and church.

Work (biblical sense): An activity viewed as an act of faith, service, and love, not merely a means to a paycheck or personal gain. It involves contributing to needs, meeting responsibilities for family and community, and reflecting love for one's neighbor, whether paid or unpaid.

Worldview: The fundamental framework through which a person perceives and interprets reality. For believers, a gospel worldview involves a "Copernican shift" from a self-centered to a God-centered perspective, profoundly influencing values, desires, and actions, and enabling a new way of seeing and living.

Wrath of God: God's righteous and holy response to sin and evil. It is not an irrational rage but a just judgment against all that is corrupt and unjust.

ABOUT THE AUTHOR

Krisan Marotta is the creator and host of Wednesday in the Word, the podcast about what the Bible means and how we know. Drawing on over forty years of Bible study and postgraduate work in biblical exegesis, she turns complex passages into clear, practical insight that empowers everyday believers to read Scripture for themselves. Krisan and her husband live in Charlottesville, Virginia, where she balances writing, podcasting, clog dancing, and delighting in the adventures of her grandchildren. Follow her books at krisan.com.